Finding Florida's Phantoms

Finding Florida's Phantoms
© 2004 Kathleen Walls

ALL RIGHTS RESERVED
No part of this book may be produced in any form,
by photocopying or by any electronic or mechanical means,
including information storage or retrieval systems,
without permission in writing from both the copyright
owner and the publisher of this book, except for the
minimum words needed for review.

ISBN 0-9742161-9-4
Library of Congress Control Number: 2004100605

First published in 2004 by
Global Authors Publications.

*Filling the **GAP** in publishing*

Edited by Kristie Leigh Maguire
Cover Art by Kathleen Walls
Author Photo by Veronica Byrd

Printed in USA for Global Authors Publications

What other authors are saying about *Finding Florida's Phantoms.*

From the Panhandle to Key West, the state of Florida offers its visitors far more than sunshine and warm temperatures during the year's colder months. Are you interested in a vacation that offers "history and mystery" as well as wonderful food, pleasant surroundings, and plenty of local color? If so, you can't go wrong with this combination travel guide and ghost story collection.

Florida, of course, has a right to more ghosts than more recently settled parts of the United States. As Author Walls points out, in 1620 when the Pilgrims reached Plymouth there was already a thriving settlement at St. Augustine. The state's paranormal riches date back even farther than that, though. The inhabitants of Crystal River State Archaeological Site's pre-historic burial mounds make their continuing presence known, as do those of the Timacuan Indian mound just north of the city in Ormond Beach.

Tragic lovers. A little girl playing jacks. A farmer who found a much easier (but horrific) way to get rid of his migrant workers than simply paying them for their labors. A doll that, imbued with its departed owner's personality, moves about its museum case and ruins the camera film of anyone who tries to photograph it. An old lady whose body left her beloved home when she died, but whose spirit continues to watch over the place with benevolent interest - except when a female guest's skirt is too short, in which case she tries to pull it lower by the hem! The ghosts that Walls describes are a varied lot, and an intriguing one. I believe I would take her advice about the places of which she says, "If you go there, it is wise to not go alone."

I would also take her advice about bed-and-breakfasts, inns, and eating establishments of all sorts. Her descriptions of these made me want to pull up stakes and head a thousand miles south, to sit on shady verandas and stuff myself with both gourmet and "plain old down home" cooking. Good reading even if you're not planning to travel soon, in other words!

Nina M. Osier author of *Love, Jimmy: A Maine Veteran's Longest Battle* and *Rough Rider* http://www.geocities.com/nina_osier/

If you thought you "knew" Florida, after reading Kathleen Wall's *Finding Florida's Phantoms* you will realize that you did not. I have been to Florida many times but it took reading this book for me to realize that there is much more to the "snowbird state" than sea, sand and sun - and Disney World. Ms. Walls takes you by the hand and leads you through the centuries of history - and ghosts - that make the beautiful state of Florida what it is today.

Kristie Leigh Maguire, author of *Desert Heat, No Lady and Her Tramp* and *Emails from the Edge*

Whether you're a Pensacola-born Floridian like me, a history buff, a ghost chaser, or you're simply planning your first vacation to Florida, *Finding Florida's Phantoms* is a must for your book collection.

Kathleen provides an enticing tour of some of Florida's best recreation spots from a fascinating historical perspective with an emphasis on the ethereal inhabitants of some the locales, historic homes and buildings.

Her book is filled with the rich history of Florida intertwined with tales of hauntings by unrequited lovers, victims of tragic love triangles, spirits of Civil War soldiers, and even the ghost of a cat.

Finding Florida's Phantoms will not only entertain you, but also entice you to search out these historic Florida haunts to experience for yourself.

James A Graves, Jr. Aftermath I: The Fight For Survival Aftermath II: The Deadly Game www.music-gms.com/author

Florida is a tourist Mecca best known for beautiful beaches and Disney World. In *Finding Florida's Phantoms*, author Kathleen Walls provides readers with a unique twist to the tired old tourist guide. Walls challenges readers to explore the "other side" of the Sunshine State – a world of legends and lore that few have explored. The book is chock-full of wonderful ghost tales interspersed with interesting Florida history and folklore. Walls also includes comprehensive tourist information on locations throughout the state such as where to stay, places to eat and unique attractions. As a Florida resident, I found the legends and history included in the volume to be quite intriguing. I also learned about some tourist spots I never knew existed. *Finding Florida's Phantoms* is a great resource for Florida natives and visitors alike and is fascinating reading even if you never venture outside your own living room.

Karen Mueller Bryson, author of *Hey Dorothy You're Not in Kansas Anymore* and *Where is Wonderland Anyway*

This a book for anyone who has ever jumped at a bump in the night, or for anyone planning on visiting the "Sunshine State". Let me make it clear. You don't have to be visiting Florida to enjoy this book, but if you visit Florida without this book, you'll be sorry.

I sat down on a Washington cold and dreary evening to review "Florida's Phantoms". Before the first chapter ended I had been carried away to white sandy beaches, crystalline waters, where headless maidens ran on the beach trying to catch up to the pirate lovers. By morning I was trying to convince my family that we really needed a warm, winter vacation in a state where we could swim with the manatee, and visit haunted buildings in the evening time.

Ms. Walls book is one that will simply have to be stocked in every gift store, in every travel agency, almost in every gas station in the country! What a travesty it would be to visit Florida without seeing some of the rare or unusual sites that so completely pack this awesome book

I had no intention of visiting Florida when I reviewed the book. Now, I have no intention of not visiting Florida and soon! I enjoyed the book for the pleasure of reading, but I learned so much about Florida and it's inhabitants that I can't wait to go and meet them for myself!

Melissa S. James author of *American Woman American Strong* and *Stolen in the Storm* both available through PageFree Publishing

Finding Florida's Phantoms

Kathleen Walls

Global Authors Publications, Inc.

For all the hard working
Convention and Visitors Bureau people in Florida
that make a travel writer's job easier.

Once more, thanks to all the crew at
GAP who make things work for all of us. Especially Kristie.
Without her help this book would have all kinds of flaws.
Also to my daughter, Veronica,
for her help and assistance.

Finding Florida's Phantoms

Table of Contents

Introduction	2
Panhandle	**3 - 18**
Pensacola Area	3
Carrabelle, Apalachicola and Florida's Forgotten Coast	11
Northwest	**19-41**
Cedar Key	19
Tarpon Springs	24
Citrus County	33
Northeast	**42 -84**
Amelia Island	42
Jacksonville and the Beaches	47
St.Augustine	55
Lake City and Gainesville	74
Central	**85-132**
Ocala	85
Daytona Beach	92
Cassadaga	99
Brevard County	103
Orlando	110
Kissimee and St. Cloud	116
Lake Wales	119
Sebring	123
Southwest	**133-158**
Tampa Bay Area	133
Fort Myers	144
Naples	151
Southeast	**159-167**
Homestead	159
Everglades	162
Keys	**168-176**
Key West	168

Finding Florida's Phantoms

Florida! The land of sunshine and wide-open beaches. But even the Sunshine State has its dark secrets. Places where centuries old spirits remain tied to earth. Beneath the façade of fun and make believe lurks the real Florida.

Settled by often cruel conquistadors, Florida was Europe's first stronghold in the New World. The blood of Spanish, French, English and Native American had stained its verdant woodlands and sandy beaches long before it became part of the United States.

Even then, greedy land barons and simple settlers battled the heat, hurricanes, insects and snakes to create the paradise we know as modern Florida. Is it any wonder that unexplainable tales and strange phenomena still remain just below the surface?

It is still a great state for explorers of the modern persuasion. But if you want to enjoy it to the fullest, it helps to have some background and history before you begin your voyage of discovery.

I have given you the bare bones of each place where I found spirits lurking. I have also included places to stay, great eateries, fun attractions and, most important, a ghostly preview. I have divided the state according to its natural geographic areas.

Now it's up to you.

Join me as we go about Finding Florida's Phantoms.

Panhandle
Pensacola

Almost from the first days of European settlement, Pensacola has abounded in spooky legends. The first white man to sail into Pensacola Bay was a one eyed Spanish explorer named Panfilo de Narvaez in 1528. He was followed by a settlement party led by Don Tristan de Luna, who arrived in the beautiful azure bay on August 14, 1559 with a thousand stouthearted colonists. But six days later, on Aug. 20th, their spirit was broken by a fierce hurricane. The terrible loss of lives and vessels caused the frightened Spaniards to cross themselves and whispers of "Devils in the Air" and "Evil Spirits" began to be heard. De Luna and the remaining colonists abandoned the colony in 1561.

Spain and France bickered over this piece of prime waterfront real estate beginning in the 16th and through the 18th century. Then in 1821, it finally became part of the United States.

Government engineers realized that they had one of the finest harbors in the world but because of the darkness and often-turbulent storms, something had to be done to make it safer.

Finally, on March 3, 1823, Congress authorized construction of the Pensacola Lighthouse. It was the first along Florida's Gulf Coast.

They temporarily dispatched the lightship, *Aurora Borealis*, but the ship's mast lacked enough height to be of any real help. In 1824 when Pensacola was incorporated and chosen as the site of the country's newest navy yard, the powers that be decided it was time for a permanent light.

Pensacola's first light was built on a bluff about 300 yards from the site of the old Spanish Fort San Carlos. This made it about 75 feet above sea level and visible for about 17 miles out to sea.

From the beginning, the lighthouse was plagued with problems. Some were easily visible to the outside world while others were secretly contained and waiting to cause a tragedy. The mariners were unhappy about the light's similarity to the Mobile light. They also felt it was not visible far enough out in the sea. The brickwork was inferior and Florida's humidity began to creep within the walls causing dampness and degeneration of the structure. The inside spiral staircase was built without a railing, making it very dangerous.

The first keeper, Jeremiah Ingraham, lived in the little red brick keeper's house alone until 1826. After two years in his lonely position, he took a bride, a local girl named Michaela Penalber. Together they raised three children.

Like the light itself, the Penalber's appeared to be a happy normal family to outsiders. In reality, they were just the opposite. It is believed Michaela stabbed her husband to death in 1840 and then remained as keeper herself until her death in 1855. Her son-in-law, Joseph Palmes, then became the keeper.

Was Michaela doomed to hear and see her victim-husband's cries in the night? No one knows. She was not in a position to complain but things went wrong with the light. That is a fact. In the late 1840s, the clockwork mechanism failed and two men had to be hired to rotate the lamps by hand, until the mechanism could be fixed. By the 1850's, complaints about the light's deficiencies caused the Corp of Engineers to construct a new taller light half a mile west of the original light.

It was first lit by Keeper Palmes on New Year's Day, 1859. However if he expected the new light to be untroubled by his father-in-law's spirit, he was wrong. To this day, visitors tell of mysterious objects flying through the air, laughter coming from unseen beings, forms appearing at windows in the uninhabited lighthouse tower, and the back door of the keeper's house is often found open when it was closed and locked. The smell of tobacco and eerie cold spots are also experienced in the house.

Ingraham's spirit is not the only one reported in the lighthouse and keeper's cottage. Permanent bloodstains are found in an upstairs bedroom of the keeper's house. No one knows for sure how they got there but since it was customary to bury drowned people near where they were found, many unknown victims lie near by. Many of the injured were taken into the keeper's house to either die or to recover.

Other factors also contribute to the lore of Pensacola's coastal ghosts. As stated earlier, the lighthouse was built near the old Spanish fort. The clash of the two cultures, Spanish and Native American, always resulted in treachery and untimely deaths for one side or the other and, in Pensacola, this was no exception.

One story tells of a Spanish soldier, Juan Alverez, who wandered away to explore with a friend. Several Indians were to guide the men. Instead, the Indians turned on the two young men and killed the friend. Juan was wounded but managed to escape and hide in the trunk of an old hollow cypress tree.

Juan evaded his pursuers but did not have the strength to get out of the tree. He died of his wounds inside it. Later settlers told of an armored ghost who appeared once a year and wandered in the area. In 1929, the old tree was cut and split. A skeleton wearing a suit of armor was found. Juan was laid to rest in a cemetery. Since then, he has not been seen again.

During the 1840's, the U.S. government built Fort Barrancas at almost the same spot as the original fort.

The forts were built partially for protection from invasion but also to defend against the pirates who found the waters of the gulf a fertile hunting ground for plunder and treasure. It is only natural that the beach area and nearby Santa Rosa Island abound with tales of buried Spanish gold and the undead phantoms that still guard their ill-gotten treasure.

According to local legends, the pirate treasure is guarded by headless ghosts who band together to protect the gold. The rumors of the gold are somewhat verified by a newspaper article in the *Pensacola Journal* on Nov. 18, 1906. The article reports one Charles Landon and party discovered several gold doubloons dated 1786 and 1792 on Santa Rosa Island. A severe hurricane the previous month had washed out a large portion of the beach.

In another *Pensacola Journal* article from July 28, 1951, a lecturer told of persistent rumors of stashed gold at San Carlos. Treasure seekers were not allowed to search for it legally because the fort is on government property.

The rumors of ships' chests filled with gold and jewels persist to this day. Of course, where you have stories of handsome pirates with easy gold, there are bound to be tales of beautiful maidens who lost their lives because of forbidden love.

One such story concerns the Legend of Ladies Walk. The story goes that a lovely young Spanish senorita fell hopelessly in love with a handsome pirate captain. The lovers met secretly on Santa Rosa Island. The maiden knew her aristocratic father would never accept the pirate as a son-in-law. Instead, he had betrothed her to a wealthy but doddering old Don.

One day as she snuck from her casa to meet her lover, her father caught her and imprisoned her in her upstairs bedroom. From the window, she watched her handsome captain pace the dunes of Deadman's Hollow. With the help of her duenna, she escaped and was rushing to her lover's arms when she was intercepted by her father's choice for her husband-to-be. He tried to embrace the unwilling girl and at that moment, her lover spied the pair. Believing his senorita faithless, the pirate drew his sword and cut off her head. He swooped her body up and threw it in Pirates' Cove.

Another version has the lovely senorita in love with a soldier. Knowing her father will never let her marry her love, she flees family and friends and lives with him in his camp. One day while he is away, she speaks to one of his comrades. After a while, she realizes she is uncomfortable with this man's attention and tells him to leave. As the offending soldier prepares to depart, he sweeps her hand to his lips in a harmless farewell salute. At just that moment, her lover burst through the forest into camp in time to witness the scene. He draws his sword and slays his comrade and, with one sweep, also beheading the golden haired young senorita.

But even after death, in both versions of the story, she tried to explain to her jealous lover. On through the centuries, people claim to see a headless woman clad in flowing white robes and carrying her bloody head with its long blond curls pacing back and forth between Deadman's Hollow and Pirates' Cove.

Another headless ghost legend revolves around the beautiful Sarah Wharton. A pirate captain, desiring the beautiful Sarah for his own, killed her father and captured his reluctant lover-to-be. Instead, she struck him across the face, putting out an eye with her ring. In pain and anger, he beheaded her on the spot. She is rumored to roam the area around Romano Street.

Kathleen Walls

Pensacola has more than its share of ghostly lovelorn senoritis. A more modern version dates from the transfer of Florida from Spain to the United States.

After the American Revolution, the British lost interest in Florida and ceded it back to Spain. In 1819 when the United States acquired the part considered East Florida of which Pensacola was the capital, the Spanish governor was slow to process the actual transfer. So much so that President Madison sent General Andrew Jackson to rush the ratification though. He succeeded in doing this in 1821.

One of Jackson's aides, Colonel Morgan, fell in love with the beautiful Senorita Carabon. Her Castilian father would have none of it. He followed the pair to Lovers' Lane at Gull Point and killed the young man with a single shot from his pistol.

Even today, there is a slight depression on the bluff near Gull Point where the young soldier was buried. His heartbroken lover planted a pine tree and visited the site daily until her own death.

Her stern father buried her elsewhere but her spirit is said to return to walk under the pines with her forbidden love. Visitors to Lovers' Lane still catch a glimpse of a ghostly gown or hear the footsteps of an invisible woman there.

Love and war are the two main reasons for a ghostly legend. While Pensacola had its chare of lovelorn maidens, it was no stranger to war.

Since the Civil War was the most devastating war America ever fought in terms of American casualties, it is no surprise that slain soldiers from that era figure in Pensacola area's ghost legends.

Throughout the war, the area around Okaloosa Country near the Yellow River just before the Alabama line was rife with soldiers from both sides. The Confederate Walton Guards were stationed at East Pass to watch for Federal ships blockading the gulf.

Federal troops on board both the *U.S.S. Charlotte* and *U.S.S. Marie Wood* foraged farms in the area for food. One night a group of Confederate cavalry encountered the federal troops. A skirmish took place that left several Union soldiers dead. They were buried in Old Bethel Cemetery just east of Crestview. Only small squares of stone without names mark their graves. But are they content in their unmarked graves or do they still try to return to the federal ships?

Many people in this area have reported seeing a "gimlet eyed officer leading a patrol of men" attempting to cross at a curve in the Yellow River at night.

There is reportedly a tree nearby with a cryptic message carved in it: the letters "CSA," a spur and rowel, an arrow pointing southeast and a gun. The tree once stood in the middle of the Blackwater River before that river changed its course. Who knows what the message was supposed to convey but perhaps it marks the way for the ghostly patrol to try once more to elude their enemy.

One of Pensacola's most visited landmarks also may have its resident spirit. Fort Pickens was built in the 1820's shortly after the United States gained East Florida. It was not until the Civil War that the fort played any significant role.

As everyone knows, the first shots in the Civil War were fired at Fort Sumter, North Carolina on April 10, 1861. What many people do not know is that, barring some bad weather, Fort Pickens might have held that dubious honor.

Finding Florida's Phantoms

When Lincoln was elected, it was obvious that the South was about to succeed. Most people recognized that this would mean war. In Pensacola, state and federal personnel worked to try and avoid the inevitable. When Florida left the union, there were four brick forts to protect the harbor and adjourning navy yard, Fort Pickens on the western end of Santa Rosa Island, Fort McRee to the west across the ship channel, and Fort Barrancas and its Advanced Redoubt on the mainland.

U.S. Army Lieutenant Adam J. Slemmer, the ranking officer at Fort Barrancas, realized that in the face of an attack, his small force of 51 men could not hold all four forts. On January 10, 1861, the day Florida seceded from the Union, he moved all of his troops into Fort Pickens, which he felt was crucial to the defense of Pensacola's harbor. Confederate soldiers took possession of the other three forts at once. On January 15th, the Confederates demanded the surrender of Fort Pickens. Lieutenant Slemmer refused. Since neither side wanted to strike the first blow, they reached a compromise. The South would not attack as long as Fort Pickens was not reinforced.

At the end of January, Federal ships with reinforcements did arrive at Fort Pickins but could not land because of the terms of the treaty. For over two months, both sides were at a standoff.

Lieutenant Slemmer knew the attack was coming. The Confederates planned a surprise attack in early April but storms kept them at bay. When they finally attacked on the 12th of April, Fort Sumner had already gone down in history and the war was on in earnest.

The Rebels tried several time to take the fort without success. Eventually they abandoned the other three forts to the Union soldiers.

Visitors to the fort today report a feeling of a presence watching you in certain rooms. Could that be one of the soldiers still keeping watch against the Confederate attackers?

Fort Barrancas also has its resident phantom, Captain Hale. Captain Hale died of yellow fever in August of 1867. His apparition was reported prowling the fort walls by no less a personage than the commandant of the entire district, Captain Henry Sanford Gansevoort. In a letter to his sister in November 1867, he reported that the sentinels patrolling the outer walls of the fort encountered the late captain. When the frighten men charged the apparition with their bayonets, it disappeared.

The old forts are not the only military buildings reputed to have resident sprits. Naval Education and Training Building, once used as a hospital, has had many reports of moving objects, doors slamming and smell of pipe smoke. There is a story that during a yellow fever epidemic, one young officer, believing the common tale that high places and rum would prevent the decease, secluded himself in a turret room. He had his meals and a glass of rum lifted to him by means of a pulley and rope. One day, he did not receive his ration of rum. It is said he died in the tower. Perhaps it is his ghost that created the disturbances here.

Many of Pensacola's old homes are also believed to harbor the spirits of their former residents. The Fordham House was built in 1875 as a present for Laura Mareno by her father when she married Dr. William Fordham. One of the last residents of her family to live in the house was Ernestine Fordham Nathan,

Laura's daughter. Ernestine died at the ripe old age of 93 in 1976, the day before Halloween. Like most of her ancestors, she was buried in St. Michael's Cemetery.

However, as the later owners of the Victorian folk cottage soon discovered, she did not rest in peace beneath her headstone. Oh no! She remained in her former home in spirit, if not in body. There she has been known to play with the jewelry and rock in her favorite chair. She has been known to open a deadbolted door and toss tools around the room. The home is now a law office but may be seen on Pensacola's Historic Society Haunted Tour.

Another Seville Square home with its permanent resident is the Dorr House at 311 South Adams Street. It was built around 1871 by Clara Barkley Dorr, the widow of Eben Walker Dorr, the first sheriff of Escambia County after it became a state. The home is a magnificent example of Greek Revival Architecture and completely furnished with period furnishings. Docents experienced objects moved around when no one could have been in the house. People have also glimpsed the figure of Clara reclining in a fainting couch at the top of the stairs.

A word of warning to ladies who are not "appropriately dressed": Mrs. Dorr is a stickler for propriety. If you are wearing a skirt she deems too short, you may feel her tugging on the hem as if to lengthen it.

If Mrs. Dorr feels like socializing with her peers, she has no problem. The Gray House just across the square has its own resident spirit. He began manifesting himself when a family with four children moved into the home. Peter and Edna Morkin at first attributed the strange noises, inexplicably opened windows and scurrying footsteps to their children but soon found out the phenomena occurred when all of the household were accounted for.

During a séance, the presence informed them he was Thomas Moristo, a sea captain who lived there from 1718 to 1803. Thomas was a bit of a womanizer. He returned home from a voyage one day to find his house partially burned and his sweetheart gone. Since then, he is very cautious about fire hazards. He once moved a flammable paint can that the Morekin's painter had left setting in the hall.

The house has belonged to businesses since the 1980's but Thomas still lets the occupants know he is around. After a security alarm system was installed, he began setting it off so many times the police got tired of answering false alarms. When the owners asked him not to do it anymore, the false alarms stopped. Thomas seems to be a friendly obliging ghost.

Several other old houses also have their own ghosts such as the Charbonier House, the Lear House and the Axelson House. Many of the otherworldly inhabitants of Pensacola's beautiful old homes are interred in St. Michael's Cemetery. And yes, you guessed it. St. Michael's is also reputed to be haunted.

Be sure to visit the Pensacola Historical Museum when you are in that city. It is housed in the Old Christ Church. It just so happens that the church has an overabundance of departed spirits still hanging around. In the early 1800's, three of the former rectors were buried beneath the church floor. Rumors flew that the remains had been disturbed by vandals searching for loot. In later years, an archaeological project unearthed the rectors' graves and discovered they had been disturbed but the remains in each grave were indeed the correct rectors. At the reburial ceremony, one student who took part in the archaeological dig reported

Finding Florida's Phantoms

seeing three rectors in the procession. He assumed they were part of the ceremony until the procession passed behind the church. When the procession came back in sight, the three rectors had disappeared. He was even more amazed to discover he was the only one who had seen the three rectors.

Although Pensacola overflows with haunted spots to visit, make sure to leave time for some fun in the sun. The beaches there are some of the prettiest in Florida, if not anywhere. Many of the spooky spots are also historically important and worth visiting for that reason alone.

Contacts:

Sam's Fun City
6709 Pensacola Blvd
(850) 505-0800

Hopkins' House (unique "boarding house" style restaurant)
900 Spring Street.

Pensacola visitor information
1401 E. Gregory Street • Pensacola, FL 32502
(800) 874-1234 • (850) 434-1234
http://www.visitpensacola.com/history.asp

Big Lagoon State Park
12301 Gulf Beach Highway
Pensacola, Florida 32507
(850) 492-1595

The Zoo
5701 Gulf Breeze Parkway
Gulf Breeze, Florida 32563
(850) 932-2229
information@the-zoo.com

Historic Pensacola
P. O. Box 12866
Pensacola, FL 32576-2866
(850) 595-5985 x100
http://www.historicpensacola.org/

Pensacola Historical Museum
115 E. Zaragosa St.
(850) 433-1559
http://www.pensacolahistory.org/museum.htm

Noble Manor Bed & Breakfast
110 W. Strong Street
Pensacola, Florida 32501
(850) 434-9544
info2@noblemanor
John & Carol Briscoe, Innkeepers

Springhill Guesthouse
903 N. Spring Street
Pensacola, Florida 32501
(850) 438-6887
(800) 475-1956
Fax: (850) 438-9075
springhillguest@bellsouth.net
Michael and Rita Widler, Innkeepers

Finding Florida's Phantoms

Carrabelle, Apalachicola and Florida's Forgotten Coast

A tiny lighthouse stands guard over a stretch of Florida's most pristine beach. Crooked River Lighthouse is a small unpretentious structure as lighthouses go. Built in 1892, the light is supported by steel beams rather than the more common round masonry tower. Once it was flanked by the keeper's house and the assistant keeper's house. Plans are afoot to replace the keeper's house and turn it into a museum so the past will not be forgotten here. However, there is someone that still struggles to keep the past alive even though he has been dead for many a year. The story goes that one keeper died here and his body wasn't found for several weeks. Now, his shadowy figure can often be glimpsed on moonlit nights working on "his" light. To get your attention even more, it is said that if you blink your headlights, he will turn the light on for you.

He isn't the only spirit in the little fishing village of Carrabelle. The newly renovated Old Carrabelle Hotel is all spruced up after a fire devastated the historic structure. The new owners, Kathy and Skip Frink, have worked hard to preserve the 1880 era home's original Key West style. While neither Skip nor Kathy has actually seen anything supernatural, they do often feel a presence. Their normally laid-back dog, Sassy, appears aware of something the human inhabitants can't see. She refuses to go in an upstairs bedroom near the back of the house. The Regatta Room has been renovated and decorated in a nautical style but Kathy pointed out the door, which has a slight bleeding effect. She explained, "We put several coats of Kilz Stain on it and then the paint but it still has a reddish color bleeding through which will not be covered. Kilz covers everything but not this door. It was not painted that red color when we bought the house. It was a dark blue. It also seems to have been kicked in at some time." She said there had been a murder committed in the house once but she was not sure of the victim. Two other people also died in the house, a former owner, Captain Langston and his wife. The captain probably died in what is now the dining room. He had fallen on reduced circumstances and during his last years had closed off all but the front two rooms. His wife, who had died years before, may have died in that upstairs room. She had suffered from agoraphobia and seldom left the house.

Strangely enough, the former owner, Mr. Vowel, also had pets that refused to go in the same room. His cats would sit and stare at the wall as if their eyes were following something that only they could see. Today, the inn is a gracious bed and breakfast.

Another old home, which has also been converted to a bed and breakfast, has its unearthly story. Amanda Marcum grew up in Carrabelle. She is now a college student but has never forgotten one frightening experience when she ventured into forbidden territory. The house involved was originally built by the Duval family in the early 1900's. During Amanda's childhood, family friends Frances and Milton Kelly occupied it. The Kelly children, David and Sheila, were not allowed upstairs. No one was. There were rumors of footsteps, a woman's voice singing a sad song and mysterious happenings in those four upper rooms. When Amanda spent a week visiting the Kelley's during the summer of 1979 for her tenth birthday, she let curiosity win out over fear and crept up the dark staircase. What happened next is still ingrained on her memory. There were four doors off the breezeway. The first three yielded nothing except old boxes, dust and a built up feeling of suspense. It was when she opened the fourth door that terror struck. "The door opened onto a small room, painted a screaming color of sky blue. There were clouds painted around the ceiling, and a faded rainbow covered one wall. There was a perfect layette of white wicker baby furniture, with eyelet sheets and blankets. A wooden rocking horse sat in the corner and teddy bears were on the shelves with other small baby toys and stacks of blankets and cloth diapers. A thin film of dust covered everything like a silent shroud. A photograph of a dark haired woman and an infant was in a silver frame on the center shelf. I went closer to look at the photograph and it flew off the shelf and landed at my feet in a tinkle of broken glass. I fled the room, careened down the stairs, and was outside under an azalea bush in what seemed like a second."

Amanda commented that some hauntings might be better left secret. For whatever reason, the two women from Tallahassee who had bought the house and renovated it as The Carrabelle House Bed and Breakfast have now closed it and placed it on the market with Anchor Realty. If you decide to purchase it, the ghosts are included at no extra charge.

Apalachicola is just a short drive over the bridge. It is famous for its oysters but there is more than seafood to be found at its most interesting hotel. Ginger Butler has worked for the Gibson Inn since 1985. She recalls many guests commenting about a presence in room 309. She recalled one instance. "One guest, when checking out, thanked her companion for covering her last night, 'It was getting chilly.' 'I didn't!' the companion replied.'"

She hastened to clarify, "They are all good stories. Like he is looking after the guest's comfort. People have frequently felt like someone brushed up against them on the stairs. Often people will be watching television and the channels will change for no reason. Most things happen in room 309. That's where Captain Willard died."

Chef Wilhelm Bogan is also familiar with the ghost at the Gibson Inn. He was the chef in the Gibson's dining room before opening his own place, Dock on the Bay, in nearby Eastpoint. In his version, Willard was in love with one of the "Gibson Girls," the two sisters who ran the hotel in the early 1900's. They were one of the earliest owners since it was built in 1907.

Finding Florida's Phantoms

"The captain would go to San Francisco to pick up cargo and be gone for about six month at a time. Then he was lost in a storm at sea. The Gibson girls were so distraught they sold the hotel. When he returned as a ghost, he stayed on in room 309. He tried to maintain the earlier spirit of the hotel. One person on checking out said, 'I didn't know you had a service where you polished people's shoes.' The clerk replied 'No, we don't.' The ghost would often take guests shoes and put them outside the door, as they did in his time, to be polished."

Chef Wilhelm even had a personal experience with Captain Willard. "We were sitting at the bar one evening and all of a sudden stuff began to be thrown down the stairs, paper towels, soap, stuff like that. Everyone ran up stairs to 205 to find the ghost had rampaged the whole room. The beds were turned over! He did a number! Nobody knows why that room."

Another great old Apalachicola house with a spirited history almost didn't survive the wreckers. The Flatauer House now houses the Gulf State Bank. David Butler, the bank's president, recalls, "My first idea when we acquired the property was to have someone move the house elsewhere; it had deteriorated so badly that it was considered an unattractive nuisance. It had been converted to apartments back in the twenties. I even took out a full page add offering it free to anyone who would take it and restore it. No takers. Then the idea of restoring it took hold. We only had one early photograph to use so we had to rely on structural analysis."

The house chronicles the story of one family. In 1908, Adolph Flatauer was on top of the world. He built a magnificent home for his family with elegant oriental carpets and elaborate woodwork. In 1919, disaster struck. His wife, Regina, died during the flu epidemic. Adolph, unable to live without her, took his own life just a few months later. Sitting in front of the beautifully tiled fireplace in their master bedroom, he shot himself. The distraught widower desired only to join his beloved, but fate was not so kind. He died of the wound but only after suffering for three days. The spot where the bullet exited his head and struck the fireplace still remains chipped. On the tile of the hearth, there is always a spot resembling a bloodstain that will not clean no matter how hard it is scrubbed.

Emily Crumb, one of the bank employees, recalled when the bank finally finished the restoration in 1982 and held an open house to proudly display their accomplishment. "Many of the Flatauer family came. Various family members told stories about the house being haunted." One person told Emily of being in the house as a child. "She said she and a friend heard a noise during the night. The two girls crept out to investigate. In the main hall, they saw an image of a man on the stairs carrying a bowl dripping with what looked like blood. They ran to get an adult to investigate and when they returned there was no man, no blood. The experience really spooked her out."

As Emily points out, most of what occurred in the house has been told to her just as hearsay but there are some things that she and other bank employees have witnessed themselves. "Frequently when we come in the morning, our desks have been disturbed. Typewriters have been overturned. Papers have been scattered on the floor."

Ghost or not, the house is a magnificent structure. It has been brought back to its original floor plan and the bank is proud to show it to visitors. The renewed woodwork is magnificent. The floors have been brought back to their original

Dead Cypress. The fireplaces and mantles are a work of art. So when you visit, be sure to stop by and congratulate David on kicking off the entire restoration boom in Apalachicola.

There is another haunted spot in the area that is also a Mecca for birdwatchers and outdoor persons, Tate's Hell. The pristine nature preserve between Carrabelle and the Apalachicola National Forest is 144,508 acres of untamed woodland and swamp inhabited by wildlife including bears, deer, wild turkey, snakes, unlimited bird life, and lots of insects. You might be fortunate enough to spot a bald eagle or Red Cockaded Woodpecker. Be cautious though or you could end up like Cebe Tate, the man for whom the place is named.

The legend recounts that Cebe Tate, a farmer who lived in Sumatra, journeyed into the woods in the late 1800's. He was searching for a panther that was killing his cattle. He followed his dogs into the dark heart of the wetlands. One by one, the panther killed all the dogs. Tate lost his shotgun when he fell into a bog and was bitten by a Water Moccasin. He wondered for days, delirious and feverish. When he finally emerged near Carrabelle, the forty five-year-old farmer's hair had turned completely white during the ten days that he spent wandering in the swamp. The only explanation he could give of his whereabouts during his sojourn in the swamp was, "My name's Tate and I've just been through Hell."

Tate's Hell is a great place to hike, canoe or bird watch. Just let someone know when you go there. Oh, and be sure to leave the name of your next to kin with a ranger, just in case.

Another tale that could curdle the blood of even the least sensitive reader centers around a circle of barren land on the west side of Timber Island. Timber Island was created by the dredging of the river to permit larger boats entrance to the gulf. The east side of the island is normal. There are several businesses there. The most interesting to visitors is the Tiki Hut, which is a great restaurant for seafood lovers. The catch is so fresh it doesn't know it's not still in the water when it reaches your plate. The Tiki Hut owners, Marlene and John Denig, acquire their seafood directly from their next-door neighbor, Pirate Landing Seafood.

Now the west side of the island is a different story. As you cross the Carrabelle Bridge, you will spot a circle of sand where nothing grows. According to Amanda Marcum, a lifelong resident, the place is known locally as "The Landing Site." Local legends claim people have disappeared there, possibly abducted by aliens. Indeed, strange lights have been seen there only to disappear before investigators can cross the bridge. There is even a story of a pair of teenaged lovers who parked there to indulge in a favorite teenage pastime. The deserted car was found later with a dead battery and a pair of panties on the back seat. No sign of the amorous couple was ever discovered.

Perhaps an incident that occurred in that area over two centuries ago is still reverberating. History records the case of a Frenchman and his lover who were shipwrecked east of St. George Island. To survive the trek towards St. Marks, they beat their slave to death with tree branches somewhere on the west bank of the Carrabelle River. Kindling a fire, they roasted the corpse's head and ate it. They smoked the remainder of his flesh and still had some left when they arrived in St. Marks.

Could "The Landing Site" perhaps refer to a different type of travelers besides space aliens?

Finding Florida's Phantoms

Carrabelle has a lot going for it besides its overabundance of ghosts. Pristine beaches, a temperate location and a low crime rate should tempt many of the snowbirds that flock to Florida to escape the winter snow up north. There are historical attractions like the World's Smallest Police Station, which has been featured on *Real People, Ripley's Believe It or Not* and the *Today Show*, and Camp Gordon Johnson Museum, which relives the little known events of the amphibious assault forces in World War 11.

A unique attraction is the Florida State University Marine Lab. It is located there because the purity of the environment creates a hospitable place for research. It is not always open to the public but be sure to visit if there is an open house when you are in the area.

Carrabelle's waterfront combines the authenticity of a working waterfront with the fun of recreational fishing and boating. The town is quite proud of its new Riverwalk. Captains like Ron Treutel and Bob McDarris will be happy to take you fishing or cruising. Lest you think all the captains are male, think again. Captain Robyn Morgan will be happy to prove different. She, or any of the other charter boat captains, will also be happy to take you to Dog Island. There is just one lodging there, The Pelican Inn, and no crowds, bridges or traffic.

For lazier water fun, try wading or just tanning at Carrabelle Beach. When all the water sports bring on a raging appetite, you have plenty of choices. Carrabelle Junction is great for breakfast or light lunch. Harry's Restaurant will also fill the bill. For a seafood dinner cracker style, it's got to be the Tiki Hut. One unique treat there is a small lobster called a bulldozer. Fried or steamed, this is something you won't soon forget. For great oysters in the rough, try the Eastpoint Oyster House and Lighthouse Raw Bar. It sets directly on the water and has several tables where you can open your own oysters or try some of the house specials.

For the night owls, there are two lounges. Wicked Willie's goes into the wee hours. It has a lively upbeat atmosphere. Harry's Bar is another Key West style nightspot. Be sure to try the Watermelon Juice. If you are there on a Friday and spot a group of ladies clustered in one area and you happen to be male, don't join them. This is the weekly meeting of the N. P. A. (No Penis' Allowed) Club. Skip, from Old Carrabelle Hotel, made the mistake of trying to sit with them. They ran him away quick. He recalls, "And I thought those women were my friends!"

It's all in good fun, however. The club raises money for worthwhile causes and gives local women an excuse for a night out.

Art lovers, be sure to visit Carrabella Cove Gallery. If you can persuade Captain Ron to show off his garden, you'll be doubly rewarded.

If you can arrange to visit Carrabelle the last weekend in April, you are in for a treat. The Carrabelle River Festival boasts food, art, music and lots of fun.

Carrabelle may call itself "The Pearl of the Forgotten Coast" but one thing is sure. Once you visit Carrabelle, you will never forget it.

Contacts:

The Old Carrabelle Hotel
(850) 697-9010

Harry's
113 St. James Ave.
Carrabelle, Fl 32322
(8500 697-3400

The Gibson Inn
www.gibsoninn.com
(850) 653-2191

Georgian Motel
www.1800motels.com
(850) 697-3410

Ho-Hum RV Park
(888) 88HOHUM

Dock on the Bay
(850) 670-8221

Sea Breeze RV Park
(850) 697-2130

Carrabelle Palms RV Park
(850) 697-2638

Carrabelle Junction
(850) 697-9550

Wicked Willie
(850) 697-8488

Camp Gordon Johnson
(850) 697-8575

Carrabella Cove Gallery
Carrabellacove@digitalexp.com
(850) 697-8984

Captain Ron
Carrabellacove@digitalexp.com
(850) 697-8984

Captain Morgan
(850) 697-9194.

Captain Bob
(850) 697-4101

Finding Florida's Phantoms

Carrabelle's old lighthouse, does a ghostly keeper still maintain it?
Photo by Kathleen Walls

Two of the Forgotten Coast's historic inns that have neither been forgotten or forsaken by their former residents. top Old Carrabelle Hotel bottom Gibson Inn.
Photos by Kathleen Walls

Northwest
Cedar Key

Several lazy brown pelicans perch on the posts of an abandoned stilt house. The birds and the weathered cypress boards are reflected in the shallow waters of the gulf. Closer in towards the end of the dock, oyster bars peer through the ripple of the waves. This is Cedar Key. Welcome to Island Time.

This is the heart of Florida's "Nature Coast" and it has everything except the crowds. This tiny artist refuge and fishing town is still a lot like what Florida use to be before the population boom. Artists were drawn to the fishing and crabbing village because of the fantastic scenery, balmy climate and breathtaking sunsets. The April Sidewalk Arts Festival draws visitors from all over. Their Seafood Festival in October also draws crowds. When you stroll along the waterfront, you are gifted with a multitude of choices. Along with the many galleries, featuring a variety of creative endeavors, you will find unique shops and food and drink establishments. You can have a quiet drink in the company of sea birds on a deck overlooking the gulf.

But beneath the unruffled surface, spirits from another time still remain. At the Island Hotel, a vintage bed and breakfast, there are several unseen (most of the time) guests from days gone by. The hotel is listed on the National Registry of Historic Places. If there were a National Registry of Haunted Place, it would surely be on that too. Since its construction in 1859, it has played host to many colorful characters. The kind of people who enjoyed life too much to leave it without a fight.

Originally used as a general store and post office, it began to collect its first ghost. Shortly before the end of the Civil War, the manager hired a nine-year-old black boy to help around the store. One day, he saw the child put something in his pocket. Believing the boy to be stealing, the manager chased him. When the manager could not find him and the boy never returned to his job, not too much thought was given the matter. Not until about a year later when workers relining the basement cistern made a grisly discovery; the skeleton of a child was found in the cistern. To this day, the spirit of that scared child still hides in the dark basement.

During the Civil War, the hotel was used as quarters for both sides, at different times of course. It is one of the Southern soldiers who has chosen to remain and stand guard just inside a door leading to a second floor balcony. This is the most frequently sighted haunt in at the hotel but definitely not the most interesting one.

Over the years, the hotel has functioned as many things. It was a brothel and speakeasy during the prohibition years. A holdover from that period seems to be the wandering soul of a prostitute. She never does any harm, just sits on the side of a guest's bed and offers a gentle kiss.

Some of the hotel's reputed thirteen ghosts departed life due to foul play.

One of these is the spirit of a former owner, Simon Feinberg. He hired a manager named W. L. Markham. Word reached Mr. Feinberg that his manager was operating an illegal whiskey still in the hotel. They met over dinner. Markham professed his innocence. Feinberg fell asleep that night and never awoke. He died of "food poisoning." It was commonly believed that Markham was poisoned. The question of Markham's innocence remained in limbo until 1999. The then owners found remains of circular copper piping that would have been used in a still hidden in the hotel. Feinberg is believed to roam the hotel, perhaps in search of Markham, but he is quite harmless towards guests.

In 1946, Bessie and Loyal Gibbs bought the then unlivable hotel and began to revitalize it. Bessie was a flamboyant hostess and drew a clientele of some of the time's most interesting guests. The Neptune Bar downstairs, so named for the mural of King Neptune, was a favorite of actor Jack Palance. Pearl Buck, Vaughan Monroe, Tennessee Ernie Ford, Francis Langford, Myrna Loy, Richard Boone and John MacDonald were some of the other notables that frequented the hotel during the Gibbs' ownership. Bessie continued to operate the hotel after Loyal's death. After her death in 1975, her spirit appears to be still residing in what was her room when she ran the hotel, room 29.

Dining in its restaurant will transport you back to the Victorian era. Bessie was the first owner to revitalize the dining room. She insisted on the freshest of everything and hired an expert chef to prepare it. Today the tradition continues.

Two museums preserve the history of the island. The Cedar Key Historic Society, located on SR 24 and 2nd St., depicts the town's development through photographs, artifacts and tools. They can also provide you with a self-guided tour of the city.

The Cedar Key State Museum is just north of the downtown area. It contains household articles, dioramas and one of the most extensive shell collections ever assembled. They also have a restored home typical of the early area settlers.

The town has a checkered history. Its location made a haven for blockade-runners during the Civil War. Because of its extensive cedar forests, it was a lumbering and pencil manufacture center for many years. A devastating hurricane leveled much of the original town in 1896.

For the best free entertainment in town, you can sit in the beach park or on the end of the pier and watch the pelicans swoop back and forth on the roof of an abandoned boathouse perched on stilts a few hundred feet from shore. If you're lucky, you might see a pair of dolphins frolicking in the waves or a few West Indian Manatees lazily turning in the water.

Finding Florida's Phantoms

Lest you think there is any lack of sophistication in the area, visit Dakotah Winery, located just north of Chiefland on Highway 19. It offers a chance to observe how wine is grown and produced in a pristine setting that offers a haven for birds and humans as well.

Max Rittgers and his son, Rob, founded Dakotah back in the mid-1980's. It was originally intended to be a you-pick-your-own grapes type operation. However, it blossomed into a full-fledged winery and is doing well. You will be pleasantly surprised at the eclectic ambience of Dakotah. Max takes a special interest in the Native American population that flourished before the white man's diseases decimated the population and the white man's technology forced the proud natives to surrender their land.

It is from this interest that an interesting story arose. Max was on spring vacation in South Dakota in 1995, relaxing and taking a canoe trip down the Cheyenne and Belle Fourche Rivers with his black Labrador, Ben. Ben unearthed an ancient lead plate believed to be a marker left by early French explorers. He was written about in the Chicago Tribune and mentioned on a PBS show.

Ben had unwittingly stirred up a can of worms for Max. Everybody wanted the plate. Historians, Native American tribal councils, the state of South Dakota and even the Feds got into the act. Max solved the dilemma by simply returning to the area via plane and tossing the valuable artifact back into the river from whence it had come.

Ben had his 15 minutes of fame and then life returned to normal. That is until Ben was struck and killed by a pickup truck on Christmas Eve, 1996.

Heartbroken, Max buried his faithful companion under a magnolia tree on the winery property. He erected a monument dedicated to all parents and children who have ever loved a dog.

This was not the end, however. Ben was special in life and in death he refused to leave before he was ready. Max claims Ben still prowls the winery grounds at night, sometimes startling roosting flocks of birds.

Cedar Key is located on a barrier island. Hwy. 24 connects it with the mainland by means of three bridges. There are dozens of other islets in the area but they must be reached by boat. The most interesting of these is Seahorse Key. It has a lighthouse, built in 1851 and abandoned in 1915. Today, it houses the University of Florida Marine Research and Environment Education Center. It was used as a military outpost and hospital and during the Civil War as a prison. It is also the highest point on the Gulf Coast, rising 52 feet above sea level. It is one of the thirteen islands designated as Cedar Keys National Wildlife Refuge. The refuge is home to a large variety of water birds and a thriving reptile population. Due to the scarcity of fresh water, there aren't many mammals on these islands. With the exception of Seahorse Key, which is closed to the public from March through June, the beaches of all the islands are open for boaters. The only island interior that is open is Atsena Ortie Key. These beaches are great places for swimming, bird watching, photography and shell collecting.

Just north of town, on Hwy 347, you can hike or drive the diverse habitats of the Lower Suwannee National Wildlife Refuge. Over 52,000 acres bisected by the famed Suwannee River compose one of the largest undeveloped river delta systems in the country. Its varied ecosystems support abundant plant and animal life. Alligator, osprey, eagle, white tailed deer and a multitude of other wildlife roam the preserve.

Shell Mound, a county park located at the south end of the refuge, is the site of an ancient Timaqua Indian mound. Shell Mound Trail crosses the midden at its 28-foot peak. From here, you have a spectacular view of the estuary and the gulf. For an almost guaranteed sighting of hosts of wading birds, ramble down the Dennis Creek Loop Trail. If you prowl the mound after dark, you might sight something else. Something far more eerie. The story goes, a young woman named Annie Simpson used to walk the area with her wolfhound. In the late 1800's, pirates used the secluded spot to bury treasure. On one of her evening walks, Annie and her dog accidentally discovered them at work hiding their ill-gotten loot. Neither Annie nor her dog was ever seen alive again. Treasure hunter claims to have found the remains of old chest and a large dog but Annie's remains have never been found. People wandering the mounds have reported seeing a beautiful girl with long dark hair accompanied by a wolfhound. Could Annie be tied to this, the last earthly spot she visited?

The park also boasts an inexpensive campground with electric and water hookups for short-term visitors. Whether you spend a day or a week on Cedar Key, the easygoing rhythms of the island will remain in your memory. It has no skyscrapers, no theme parks or no huge enterprises. It just has a timeless natural beauty and friendly atmosphere that will bring you back time and time again. This quaint village is one of the few places left where you can glimpse the Florida of another time.

Contacts:

Island Hotel & Restaurant
373 2nd Street · P.O. Box 460
Cedar Key, Florida 32625
(352) 543-5111
(800) 432-4640
Fax (352) 543-6949
TIH@islandhotel-cedarkey.com

Chamber of Commerce at:
info@cedarkey.org
 PO Box 610
Cedar Key, Florida 32625
(352) 543-5600

Cedar Key Historical Society
(352) 543-5549

Cedar Key RV Park is located in town. It is a short walk from downtown and is on the gulf.

Finding Florida's Phantoms

Rainbow Country RV Campground
Hwy 24
543-6268

Dakotah Winery,
14365 NW Hwy. 19
Chiefland, FL 32626
(352) 493-9309

Tarpon Springs

America is known as the great melting pot. Occasionally, a group of immigrants settle an area and do not blend into the great homologous masses. Instead, that town becomes a tiny enclave of the mother country.

Tarpon Springs, on the gulf coast of Florida, is such a place. Its culture is as Greek as any Aegean Island. As you stroll down Dodecanese Boulevard, the honey-sweet aroma of Baklava wafts from the Parthenon or Hellas Bakeries. The sharp tang of Feta Cheese assails you from Louis Pappas Restaurant. In Plaka Restaurant, you watch as a swarthy man expertly carves lamb from a slowly revolving spit to create a mouthwatering gyro.

A gentle sea breeze plays a tinkling tune on the seashell mobiles and sways the dangling lines filled with freshly harvested sponges. The mournful sound of a Greek love song drifts from the courtyard of what was once the old Sponge Exchange, now converted into upscale boutiques, gift shops and food and drink establishments. Inside the gleaming whitewashed walls, tables are arranged so you can rest from your sightseeing and sip a glass of Retsina or nibble on a flaky pastry as you enjoy the music of The Islanders.

On one side of the courtyard stands a refurbished sponge diving ship, the Aegean Isles. Her smart black and red trim stand out in sharp contrast to her sparkling white hull.

On a front wall of the Sponge Exchange, there is a huge Byzantine style painting of a sponge diver. At the bottom right of the picture is a small plaque. It reads "In memory of John M. Cocoris from Leonidion, Greece. The founder of the sponge diving industry in 1905 in the city of Tarpon Springs."

These two displays encapsulate the Greek heritage of Tarpon Springs. When a Greek sponge diver named John Cocoris, arrived in Tarpon Springs in 1905, it was a winter vacation town for wealthy Northerners seeking respite from the bitter cold. When he discovered the quality and extent of the sponge beds in the Gulf of Mexico, he sent out an invitation for many of his compatriots to join him in harvesting the beds. They came with their families and found these beds even more lucrative than the ones in Greece. Boats like the Aegean Isles, over two hundred of them in the heyday of the 1930's, crisscrossed the shallow gulf waters

Finding Florida's Phantoms

in search of their quarry. These intrepid divers wore full dive suits and helmets with an air hose attached to the compressor on the boat. They weighed their bodies down with heavy weights.

For their risks, they were amply rewarded, bringing in as much as three million dollars a year of the sponges. Then in the 1940's, tragedy struck. A bacterial infection declaimed most of the beds. It wasn't until the 1980's that new healthy beds were discovered and the divers began again exporting the finest natural sponges in the world. Tarpon Springs is still a leader in the world's market but that market is greatly reduced due to the introduction of synthetics. However, the romance and culture of the divers are still an integral part of this colorful city. No synthetic "tourist attraction" can create the vibrancy that exists in Tarpon Springs.

Today, you can board the St. Nicholas at the sponge dock and observe an authentic sponge dive. This is a great way to get the feel of the place. The boat is not just a tour boat, although those are available, too. It's a genuine sponging boat. The young diver dons an old-fashioned diving suit and heavy iron helmet. His air line lies across the deck as he descends into the water is search of a living sponge. You hold your breath while he is down. Soon, he signals to be raised. He breaks the surface and holds aloft a real sponge.

As you amble the weathered boards of the old docks, you can glimpse what life was really like here in the early 1900's. Whether you take a cruse, go deep-sea fishing, tour the salt-water aquarium, visit the Spongeorama, or view the movie about the sponge diving industry, you realize life here was geared to the sea. Even here, the old spirits are thought to be still stirring. Objects seem to mysteriously move themselves and strange noises in the Spongeorama remind folks that by day this museum may throng with tourists, but at night it is still the domain of the long departed souls of the old spongers.

The swooping gulls, the salt spray of passing boats and even the tangy salt smell of the breeze remind you of that. As mysticism runs strong in the Greek culture, you would expect this charming little city to boast unexplained events and you won't be disappointed

The spiritual heritage of the early Greeks is embodied in the St. Nicholas Cathedral. This church was built first in 1908. A later classic Byzantine church was begun in 1941. It was designed as a replica of St. Sophia of Constantinople, one of the most beautiful of all the Greek Orthodox churches. Other than drawing visitors to gawk at its beauty and worshipers to pray, it has become famous as the home of the "weeping" icon of St. Nicholas.

The Weeping Icon is a picture of the church patron, St. Nicholas. On Dec. 5, 1970, a cleaning woman noticed something strange about the holy picture. The icon began to shed tears. A carpenter called to examine the frame for possible moisture leaking into it declared the frame air tight, yet the moisture still accumulated and rained down the saint's painted face. The phenomena continued until Dec of 1973 when it stopped abruptly.

For a while, the controversy as to whether a miracle had occurred diminished.

Then in August of 1992, the saint once more began to cry. He continued until February 1996 and again abruptly stopped. Many people witnessed the tears during the two periods. Today, the tracks are still visible to all who visit the church.

Kathleen Walls

The situation is made even stranger by the stories of yet more weeping icons. Sandwiched between two houses on Hope St, there is another icon and a shrine with a miraculous history. The Shrine of St. Michael was built in response to a miracle. Originally, the icon came from Greece to the home of the Tsalichis family in 1937.

Its miraculous history began early and, some believe, continues to this day. The first warning that the icon was unusual began when the owner and several of her friends heard the sound of church bells emanating from it. She took it to the parish church where a special blessing was held. The bells continued over the next two years.

Then in December of 1939, little Steve Tsalichis took sick. The doctors could not find a cure for what was thought to be a brain tumor and it was feared the worst would happen to the sick eleven-year-old. The child requested the icon and his mother laid it on his chest. Miraculously the boy was cured. He told his mother that St. Michael wanted a shrine built in his honor. Within two years, Mrs. Tsalichis completed the shrine and enthroned the icon within.

Word of the healing spreads and many of the faithful visited the shrine and claimed a cure. Then something else strange and wonderful happened again. This time it didn't start with the icon of St. Michael but one of other icons in the shrine. On July 18, 1989, Rita Koutsourais, a local shopkeeper, was praying at the shrine when she noticed something unusual. The icon of the Blessed Mother seemed to be crying. The shrine has had a reputation of producing many healings but this time the news spread like wildfire. Over three thousand people thronged to the shrine before the phenomena ended. Within days, seven of the other icons were weeping. A local priest preformed services daily for the multitudes at the tiny chapel. Eventually the weeping ended and the crowds ceased but the faithful still come to the tiny shrine looking for a miracle. According to Mrs. Tsalichis, who died in 1994 at the age of 88, she can recall healings attributed to the shrine. She tells of a deaf woman who regained her hearing and a crippled woman who was able to walk again. Her own son, Steve, continued to enjoy good health and is a thriving restaurateur in Tarpon Springs.

Was there a meaning or a purpose for the tears of any of the icons? I have no idea. Neither has anyone else come up with any reason or explanation. Many have tried to debunk the story, especially the happenings at the shrine of St. Michael. But the fact that so many people observed all of the occurrences make it difficult to doubt that something out of the realm of the normal happened more than once in this in the quiet little town.

But here and there, you see clues that this peaceful little town wasn't always so sedate. The colorful flower of today's Tarpon Springs grew from some very thorny roots. There are those who say one of the town's toughest lawmen has never left his beat. Ask any of the town's older residents about "The Badge" and you will hear the story of Rube Jones.

Rube was a lawman cut from the same cloth as the Wild West legends like Wyatt Earp and Pat Garrett. Some say he used his gun too freely. Some say he walked on both sides of the line dividing "lawman" from "outlaw." No one disputes the claim that he was the most memorable Marshall in Tarpon Spring history. He stood well over 6 feet tall and carried a shotgun as well as a sidearm. He was known for warning a lawbreaker once and shooting him the second time. He shot

Finding Florida's Phantoms

one man who dared to run against him and beat the case in court claiming self-defense. Needless to say, he won the election. In fact, he won twelve elections from 1906 to 1918. He wore a gold badge made from two Double Eagles, a twenty-dollar gold coin. Tales are told of Rube picking up the town's prostitutes in Tampa and making sure they left town after they concluded their business. Each month, Rube would enter the sheriff's office with a pocket full of bills collected from "fines" levied against the prostitutes.

At the same time, Rube was very protective of the Greek community that was arising in Tarpon Springs. Many of the rowdier citizens thought it was a lark to beat up the new immigrants. Jones refused to let that happen, thus earning the trust and respect of the divers and their families.

When the office became appointive rather than elective, Rube "resigned" but true to the gunslinger's style, he didn't fade quietly away. No! Not Rube! He was gunned down in his car along with a friend. There were so many bullets in him he was barely recognizable. Evan after his death, the legend of his ghost haunting the town to "get wrongdoers" was an accepted story. Rube is buried in the town he guarded in Cycadia Cemetery. Does he rest in peace there or does his restless spirit still search for the men who gunned him down and never got caught?

Speaking of cemeteries, there is another old graveyard that ghost hunters need to visit in Tarpon springs. It is the Rose Cemetery on US 19 and Tarpon Springs Ave. just across the street from Cycidia Cemetery. Unlike the well-maintained Cycidia, this one is in sad shape. It is called Rose Cemetery and is a relic of the days of racial segregation. Rose is a black cemetery going back about a hundred years. The city is currently trying to provide funds to maintain and restore the old graveyard. Visitors there at night tell of large floating orbs and strange noises. A local ghost hunter group conducted an investigation there and reported many presences. It is not just in the places of the dead that souls of the departed linger.

On Riverside Drive, the old Anclote Manor mental hospital's peaceful façade hides many evils and perhaps more than one troubled spirit. The building has had many incarnations, most of them ended badly.

It began life in 1928 as The Sunset Hills Country Club. One of its most infamous guests was Al Capone. But as the rich and famous found newer playgrounds, it was shut down in the mid 1900's.

In 1953, it reopened as a psychiatric hospital. During that time, Anclote Manor was referred to in local newspapers as "a medieval house of horrors." It was rumored that patients were tied to their beds and cruel and unnecessary operations were preformed on them. The name was changed to Northpointe Behavioral Health System in 1996, perhaps because the previous year it had been cited by the state for violation of laws regulating detention of patients.

Several of the administrators of the hospital eventually were found guilty of fraud and were sentenced. The old resort is still looking for a new owner as of Feb 2003. There had been many projects proposed for it but somehow they were all doomed to fail. The latest was a series of townhouses planned by a Miami developer. That plan fell by the wayside when angry local residents objected to the increased density in their residential neighborhood. Perhaps the spirits that inhabit the old buildings prefer their privacy.

Visitors to the deserted complex still claim to see people in white who disappear and hear strange noises. Skeptics might dispute the presence of the long dead but they cannot deny that a lot of strange circumstances seem to conspire to keep the place in its current deserted state. Two local residents, Chelsea Mihall & Henry de la Vega, visited The Manors to determine for themselves if there was any truth to the stories. Chelsea related their experiences.: "Almost everyone who goes to check out The Manors has an interesting story to come home with. Stories of slamming doors, lights switching on and off, and seeing different things. We decided to go there and see if anything weird would happen to *us*. When we were by the Physicians Building, we saw a person in a white shirt walk behind a pole and never come out of the other side. We also heard lots of noises and voices coming from the inside, and just had an overall sense of being watched. There are also lights on in various different rooms at different times during the day."

The Manors has remained on the market after the hospital declared bankruptcy in 1997. It has had its share of potential buyers but for one reason or another, things never went smoothly. Only time will tell if its latest project will materialize.

Of course, there are other things to do here besides visit cemeteries and seek otherworldly visitors. If you're a gambler, the new state of the art floating casino may tempt you to court Lady Luck. There are restaurants in abundance. They vary from the elegant Louis Pappas, with its three dining rooms overlooking the Anclote River, to the unusual Lighthouse Restaurant.

Take time to stroll through the many small shops on Dodecanese Boulevard and along the side streets. Aside from the sponges, you'll find many unusual items such as embroidered Greek blouses and amber colored kombolis, Greek worry beads. The shop owners are friendly and proud of their heritage. They enjoy explaining their culture to visitors. Stray a bit off the main streets for a glimpse of the homes with their colorful flowers and unique design.

Tarpon Springs has several parks you will want to visit. At Sunset Beach, toss your burgers onto a smoldering grill then sit back and watch the waves break on the sandy beach. You can take a dip or launch your boat here, too.

Fred Howard Park is another scenic gulf beach. This 150-acre county park has a mile long causeway connecting the swimming area with the mainland. It also has barbecue grills, shelters, fishing spots and restrooms.

If you're not interested in swimming, A.L. Anderson Park is a great place for picnicking or fishing and boating. It's located on Lake Tarpon to the east of the city.

For a different close to nature feeling, try Highland Nature Park. This small city park focuses on the natural beauty of the area's foliage.

Hikers and bikers will savor a trip along the Pinellas Trail. This winding path extends from St. Petersburg to Tarpon Springs. It's a great way place to walk off the excess pounds Greek cuisine tends to add.

For music buffs, there is an unusual haunted spot, Studio 420. The state of the art music-recording studio is located incongruously in a 1905 Victorian home that was used first as a hospital by Dr. Douglas. In one of the upstairs rooms, a young girl named Elizabeth died in childbirth. Perhaps she is still hunting the unborn child or just unable to believe she died in giving life. Whatever her reasons,

Finding Florida's Phantoms

she must like modern music since she is still hanging around the studio located at 420 E Tarpon Ave.

Elizabeth isn't the only free spirit hanging around the studio. There are at least two other ghosts. One likes an upstairs fireplace and one prefers an area near the attic. They are especially active after a.m..

One musician, Jonathan Hay, who works and records at the studio, had some unusual encounters. He explains how he came to meet Elizabeth. "I began working at Studio 420 in 1999 when I was fortunate enough to land a production deal, meaning I'd receive free studio time and Studio 420 would produce all of my material. Periodically, over a span of about two years, I stayed at the studio while working on a hip-hop album for my group, Audio Stepchild. I chose Studio 420 because Larry Greenbaum (Puff Daddy, Bad Boy camp, Wu-Tang Clan) was the engineer and I knew I could use the credits.

During the first month of work, I heard constant rumors of the studio being haunted by ghosts, as the building is a former hospital. I could say that from time to time I'd feel an odd energy about the building, but I left short of any strange occurrences."

Jonathan left the job for a few months then returned a few months later. "I continued to hear rumors and no sooner had I settled in did I experience my own encounters.

The first unsettling experience I had was while tracking a song, featuring Prince, *When Will We Be Paid?* and a door slammed upstairs, however everyone in the building was in the downstairs room, recording. We paused the track to listen further and heard footsteps scrambling down the stairs and suddenly stopping. Then there was silence. The music started up again as if everyone was used to hearing such noises, but I was very uneasy. The more time I spent at the property, the more noises I heard, and I learned that people do just get accustomed to all the creaking, the footsteps, the doors slamming because it is constantly happening."

His partner in Audio Stepchild, Jason Eisenmenger, was a skeptic of the paranormal until one afternoon while both men were outside the front door taking a break, when conversation of the ghost that haunts the studio began. Jason proclaimed that he did not believe in ghosts. Then something strange happened. "The front doorbell of the building promptly rang. He asked if I had rung the bell, which of course I had not, and once I assured him of that, the bell rang again even though no one had pushed it.

This next instance I could possibly chalk up to my eyes playing tricks on me but I'll never be completely sure. I had been sleeping on the downstairs sofa and was jolted awake by the feeling of being watched. I could see a vague figure of a woman at the top of the staircase. Knowing that only one other person was in the building, I called for him and once he headed down the stairs, the figure vanished."

There is another instance when Jonathan definitely saw something. "After completing a rough mix (a reference CD used as a basis before the final product is made) of some of our songs, I headed outside to listen to it on the studio owner Matt Gullo's truck. While listening, I was glancing around at the scenery. I suddenly felt very secluded because even though the studio is in a neighborhood, the rear is surrounded by trees. The sun had begun to set so it was not as bright and my eyes drifted over to the upper-right window of the studio. A woman was standing there, looking out at the sunset. She looked as though she had an almost phosphoric glow about her. Confused and slightly frightened, I honked the horn to get someone's attention. Levin Venson, a member of the production crew who happens to reside next door to the studio, quickly came to see what was the matter. I told him about the woman I saw and he informed me that people at the studio see her all the time. She is the ghost that haunts the building and her name is Elizabeth.

I never could go into the CD duplication room by myself, that being the room I saw that woman in from the truck. There is a presence I simply can't explain."

He is not the only one at the studio to have encounters with Elizabeth. "The last instance I'd like to share is one that did not happen to me but to the engineer, Larry Greenbaum. Larry was mixing a song called *Bizarre*. His eyes and ears were heavily fatigued, but with a deadline on his shoulders, sleep would have to wait. Larry was cautious to lock each and every door, knowing that with a bar two doors down, it is not uncommon for drunks to wander in the studio and make themselves at home. Larry was trying to focus on the task at hand when he felt an unmistakable tap on his shoulder. Looking at a computer monitor for the mixing process, Larry tried to make out a reflection of who had tapped him, without having to turn around. He could not. When Larry turned around, there was no one there. Larry called out to see if there was anyone in the building, but he already knew that he was alone. Larry ran from the building as fast as he could and called me on the phone to tell me of his experience."

Jonathan has since left Studio 420 to work with the multi-platinum Days of the New and later working on the Lucy Diamonds project. He will be doing some of her work at Studio 420. Asked how he feels about that, he replies, "I am excited about spending some time with my friends over at 420, even the friends that aren't..."

If you only visit one nightspot, make it Zorba's. On weekends, you will be treated to a genuine belly dancer. Inside the dusky club, with the strident sound of the bouzouki beating in your eardrums, it's easy to imagine yourself transported, in time as well as space, to a Mediterranean Bazaar. To further the illusion, the local men often perform an impromptu version of the syrtaki or one of the other traditional male dances.

The historic downtown section located several blocks southeast of the Docks has been named a National Historic District. This was the original business district of Tarpon Springs, predating the arrival of the Greek divers. It has been restored to its former glory, circa 1880. The nostalgic brick sidewalks with their quaint green benches and old-fashioned gas-style street lamps have drawn a diverse collection of artistic studios, unique shops, Bed and Breakfasts and restaurants. Nearby, the restored homes of many of the earlier city founders add diversity to the Hellenic influence of the homes near the Docks.

Tarpon Springs is big on festivals. Almost any time of the year is an excuse to celebrate. One of the more unique events is the January observance of the Epiphany. It begins as a religious celebration, then stages a diving competition among the young boys to retrieve a cross tossed into the waters of Spring Bayou. Greek dancing, music and food are provided. This event draws over 20,000

Finding Florida's Phantoms

annually. The Taste of Tarpon Festival, held on the Docks in March, pays homage to the towns restaurants with creative cookery as well as arts and crafts. The arts do have their hour in the sun with the two Arts and Crafts Festivals, held in April and November.

Of course, September's fishing tournament is a big deal for fishermen from all over. Several other festivities are held including Christmas and Halloween celebrations.

Tarpon Springs is often called the "Venice of the South" because of its many bayous and lakes. Altogether, it has over fifty miles of waterfront.

A visit to Tarpon Springs is a great way to experience "The grandeur that was Greece," without ever leaving our own great country. However, its ghosts are All-American.

Contacts:

Sponge Docks
Dodecanese Blvd
Tarpon Springs.
(727) 942-6381.

St. Nicholas Boat Line
693 Dodecanese Blvd.,
Tarpon Springs.
(727) 942-6425

Spongeorama
510 Dodecanese Blvd.,
Tarpon Springs.
(727) 942-3771

Tarpon Springs Aquarium
850 Dodecanese Blvd.,
Tarpon Springs.
(727) 938-5378

St. Nicholas Greek Orthodox Cathedral,
36 N. Pinellas Ave.
Tarpon Springs.
(727)937-3540.

Pappas Restaurant
10 W. Dodecanese Blvd.,
Tarpon Springs.
(727) 937-5101.

Spring Bayou Inn
32 W. Tarpon Ave.
Tarpon Springs.
(727) 938-9333

Fred Howard Park
West end of Sunset Drive,
Tarpon Springs.
(727) 943-4081

Sunset Beach
West end of Gulf Road,
(727) 942-5628

Tarpon Springs Chamber of Commerce
(727) 937-6109.

Studio 420
420 Tarpon Ave.

Citrus County

Each winter thousands of visitors flock to Florida's Citrus County. They come by road or air, but the most interesting visitors are the ones that come by water. West Indian Manatees come to here in the winter for many of the same reasons that the humans do, mild winters and warm waters for swimming.

Citrus County's main draw as one of the state's most unique vacation spots is due to this ungainly mammal and, in return, the county takes good care of their huge aquatic guests. Forty six percent of the county has been set aside for parks and preserves and special manatee sanctuaries have been set up in the waters of Crystal River, Chassahowitzka River, Kings Bay and the other waterways frequented by the sea cows.

These creatures are huge. Manatees usually weigh from 1,000 to 1,500 pounds. The female only gives birth to a single calf once every two to five years. Occasionally they have twins. The mothers seem to teach their newborn calf and tend it for several years, thus the long spacing between births. This low birthrate combined with man's careless use of boats is the main reason manatees are so endangered.

Newborn calves suckle milk like all other mammals until they are several months old, then they begin feeding on vegetation. Like elephants, their closest relation, they grow all their lives. One thirteen foot plus manatee was weighed in at 3,200 pounds

They are very social animal and frequently are found in large groups grazing and playing. Like all mammals, they must breathe air. It is when they must surface, at least every fifteen minutes, that they are in the gravest danger of being struck and injured by fast turning boat propellers. It is for this reason that "Slow Speed Zones" are so important if this fascinating animal is to have a chance at survival

There is no thrill on earth like snorkeling with these gentle giants. Their playful personality and curious nature bring them right to your side. Their great size is never a threat as they are total pacifists. An interesting story told by an attendant at the Homosassa Springs Wildlife Park, one of the best places to study the sea mammals up close, tells of a manatee and shark encounter. The park houses a permanent herd of manatees that for one reason or other cannot be returned to the wild. One winter, a shark made its way into the enclosed area with the manatees. Keepers feared for the manatees' safety. The manatees, however, had no fear of this predatory creature. They swam up to it and proceeded to play. The shark must have been confused by the antics of the manatees since it never attempted to harm them.

The manatees in the park are so acclimated to their human attendants they actually swim up and take carrots out of their hands at show time. The park is reached by way of a pontoon boat that takes you from the entrance on highway 19 on a short voyage through the wildlife sanctuary. If you are lucky, you will spot deer, raccoons, otters and other wildlife that share the park with the manatees.

Once inside the park, you can study the huge bewhiskered sea cows in their natural habitat, underwater. The park boasts an underwater observatory where you can even hear the manatee sounds via telephones. The giant salad bowl for the manatees is always filled with fresh romaine lettuce so you can observe the giant cows doing what they enjoy most, munching on a snack.

After you have learned about the fun-loving mammals, the next step is to join one of the snorkeling expeditions and actually get into their environment to play with them. Plantation Inn Dive Shop has a good program. You can rent all the equipment you need and the experienced guides will help you become acclimated to the mask and other equipment if you are new to this type of thing. Incidentally, the Plantation Inn has a great buffet if all the water activity has worked up an appetite.

The Ramada Nature Coast Resort is located next to the entrance to the wildlife park. They have another great restaurant located there. The Riverside Buffet offers Cracker Cooking at its best. Chef Charley Brown is a native who grew up appreciating the dishes he now offers. One taste and you will appreciate them too.

There is even a two-day Manatee festival, which honors Citrus County's favorite mammal. You can enjoy a boat tour on the beautiful Kings Bay for a small charge and most likely spot a few of the gentle mammals.

Of course, there will be other activities at the festival. You can find anything from watercolor artwork to breathtaking photography, sculptures, stained glass and unique one-of-a-kind handmade jewelry. What is a festival without music? Live entertainment will be provided continuously during the event. The festival will also offer their third annual Jimmy Buffet sound-a-like contest

One other eco-based facility to visit there is the Marine Science Station. The station is officially part of the school system in the county but they do offer a lot more than classes. Pat Purcell, the soon to be retired director of the program, envisions the center as teaching both adults and children the importance of the area's ecosystem. Tours can be arranged through the center for small or large groups. This is a once in a lifetime chance to see the inhabitants of the waterways and marshes of Citrus County close up.

But if you have come to see ghosts, not huge aquatic mammals, you are still in the right place. Beneath the nature-loving exterior of Citrus County, there are many esoteric haunts and I do mean haunts.

Interestingly, the first humans who left evidence of their habitation of the Crystal River area were also seasonal visitors. They migrated to make the best use of mostly aquatic resources. Archaeologists believe these people of the Deptford Culture inhabited the area around 500 BC to 300 AD and were the first to begin building the mysterious mounds in western Citrus County.

These original tribes were followed by increasingly advanced cultures that flourished until about the time Columbus began his fateful journey of discovery.

The Crystal River State Archaeological Site with six mounds dating back to pre-historic times is worth a visit. An unusual feature of the site is two upright ceremonial stones, or "stelae," one with the likeness of a human head carved on its surface

These mounds the early people left behind, temple and burial mounds, point to an increased level of ceremony and social development. Pottery, copper artifacts and tools were often buried with the dead.

But did these dead always stay in their Happy Hunting Grounds? There is evidence that says not. One of the rangers, Mrs. Clemons, has heard voices at the mounds many times when there is no other living person around. Others have claimed to see beings floating above the ground at the site.

When thoughts turn towards food, K.C. Crumps is a local tradition from way back. It has a long and spirited history. Its history dates back to the 1890's. The Silver Springs, Ocala and Gulf Railroad Company completed an extension of its Ocala to Dunnellon line in 1887. This extension went from Dunnellon to Homosassa and opened up the area to tourist. One of the most illustrious winter visitors was President Grover Cleveland. He made his winter headquarters at Crumps Lodge.

No one is sure when the strange things began happening. However, there is no denying that there is some unearthly presence still here. Lights come on and the figure of a seaman is seen in windows.

One of the employers was working in an upstairs room late one night. The restaurant was closed and he was working on the books when he heard the television go on downstairs. He went down and turned it off. No sooner did he sit back down and return to his figures than he heard the television come back on full blast. He decided it was time to quit for the night and let "the presence" have free run of the place.

As I was leaving, I stopped to speak with one of the housekeeping staff. She told me she had also had an encounter with the spirit. "I was sweeping in the little room with the fireplace. I felt something swoosh just behind and turned and felt someone brush past me. No one else was in the room. At least no one I could see."

The restaurant closed down for a while in 2003 but is now reopened. So be sure to ask the new owners, Byron and Cindy Rogers, if they have had any encounters with their resident spirit.

There are lots of other attractions in the area too. Yulee Sugar Mill Ruins State Historic Site is a well-preserved ruin that includes original remains of the boiler, chimney and mill machinery of an old sugar mill.

If you need some indoor activities to balance all the natural attractions, you will find plenty to do as well. Just across the street from the sugar mill ruins, you will find the Olde Mill House Gallery and Printing Museum, a museum dedicated to the history of printing from Gutenberg through the early 1900's.

The Ted Williams Museum lets you can relive moments from the "Splendid Splinter's" life. The 1912 Old Citrus County Courthouse, listed on the National Register of Historic Places, is also famous for the courtroom featured in the 1961 Elvis Presley film, *Follow That Dream.*

Since we, unlike the manatees, need a place to stay on dry land, why not make it a special adventure? Rock Crusher Canyon is one of Florida's newest hidden attractions. It opened in October of 1999 near Crystal River. An old limestone quarry forms the canyon and its 90-foot cliff creates Florida's largest natural amphitheater. It seats 7,500 people for the concerts, which run the gauntlet from "Golden Oldies" to Country and Western. In addition, the Canyon features entertainment in the Garden Pavilion. Some of the canyon's events read like a "Who's Who" of the biggest names in the entertainment business: Willie Nelson, Danny and The Juniors, Mickey Rooney, Herman's Hermits, Loretta Lynn, Faith Hill, The Sammy Kaye Orchestra and many other equally famous entertainers. Florida Cracker Style buffets are usually included in the price of the show, which range from $15 to $40.

The Crystal River Jam, one of Florida's most popular two-day outdoor country music events, is held annually each November at the amphitheater. The concerts and entertainment are open to the general public but special prices are offered for campers.

About once a month, the park features a Sunday brunch with live entertainment. Luncheon shows featuring the canyon's in house group, Razz Ma Tazz, are also offered.

The campground has 400 sites. All have full hookups plus cable TV, Internet and instant phone service. The clubhouse features a large pool, whirlpool and exercise facility. There are laundry and limited groceries on site. They welcome jamborees, RV rallies, weddings, banquets and other large groups as well as the individual camper

Campers can enjoy an emerald green lake for swimming, fishing or paddleboat rentals.

Another way to get up close and personal with not only the manatees but also the areas other abundant wild life is on one of the many river cruises. Captain Mike's Lazy River Cruises is an excellent one.

If you feel more energetic, you might try Riversport Kayaks. Depending on your skill level, they offer many different options for kayaking on Citrus County waters. If a complete novice like myself was able to enjoy a five-mile trip and not even feel sore the next day, anyone can do it. . Here you will encounter lots of bird life and possibly spot a manatee or two. Of course, manatee watching is just one of the many experiences the Florida's Nature Coast offers so, why don't you go play with the manatees in Citrus County in between your ghost hunting?

Finding Florida's Phantoms

Contacts:

Citrus County
1-800-587-6667
visit@citrus.infi.net
www.visitcitrus.com

Rock Crusher Canyon
1-877-RC-Canyon
www.rockcrushercanyon.com.

Manatee festival
January US Hwy 19 & Citrus Avenue in Historic
Downtown Crystal River
Festival Hours
Saturday 10 a.m. - 4 p.m.
Sunday 12 Noon - 4 p.m.

Marine Science Station,
12646 W. Fort Island Trail,
Crystal River, Florida 34429,
352-795-4393

Homosassa Riverside Resort
5297 South Cherokee Way
Homosassa, FL 34448

Contact: Gail Oakes
(800) 442-2040
Fax: (352) 628-5208
info@riversideresorts.com
www.riversideresorts.com

Plantation Inn and Golf Resort
9301 West Fort Island Trail
Crystal River, FL 34429

Contact: Shay Baranowski
(800) 632-6262
piresort@plantationinn.com
www.plantationinn.com

Riversport Kayaks
5297 S. Cherokee Trail
Homosassa, FL 34448
(352) 628-2474
www.flakayak.com

River Safaris
5290 S. Cherokee Way
Homosassa, FL 34442
(352) 628-5222
www.riversafaris.com

Matt Clemons
Aardvark's Kayak Co.
(352) 795-5650

K. C. Crumps
11210 West Halls River Road
Homosassa, FL

Coastal Heritage Museum
532 Citrus Avenue
Crystal River, FL 34428
(352) 795-1755

Historic Courthouse Museum
1 Courthouse Square
Inverness, FL 34450
(352) 637-9927

Naber Kids Doll Factory
8915 South Suncoast Boulevard
Homosassa, FL 34446
(352) 382-1001

Olde Mill House Gallery & Printing Museum
10466 Yulee Drive
Homosassa, FL 34487
(352) 628-1081

Ted Williams Museum & Hitters Hall of Fame
2455 North Citrus Hills Boulevard
Hernando, FL 34442
(352) 527-6566

St Nicholas Cathederal in Tarpon Springs
Photo by Kathleen Walls

Top: The Island Hotel in Cedar Key
Photo by Martin Walls
Bottom: Display honoring the early divers in Tarpon Springs
Photo by Kathleen Walls

Finding Florida's Phantoms

Top: Old Sugar Mill Ruins in Citrus county.
Bottom: Stele 2 in Crystal River Archeological Site.
Photos by Kathleen Walls

Northeast
Amelia Island

The history of Amelia Island is so colorful and its buildings so significant to Florida's past that a 50 block area downtown in its main town, Fernandina Beach, is listed on the National Register of Historic Places.

Nestled up against the Georgia border just north of Jacksonville, it was originally named in honor of Princess Amelia, the daughter of England's King George II. For over 400 years, it was fought over by Spain, France, England and finally the United States. Pirates and smugglers used it as a refuge.

The United States made its first attempt to secure the island on March 17, 1812. President Monroe "encouraged" the self-styled Patriots of Amelia Island to rebel against Spain, take over the island and then cede it to the U.S.

Of course, Spain protested and the United States had to relinquish its claim. Two later takeovers also failed. Sir Gregor MacGregor was the first but he gave it up when he ran out of money.

Then Luis Aury, a Mexican revolutionary, named himself Supreme Commander of Amelia Island and raised the Mexican flag. He, too, was forced out in December 1817. Finally in 1821, Spain ceded Florida to the United States. Amelia has been part of the United States ever since, except for when Florida seceded from the Union during the Civil War.

Luis' son, Luc Simone Aury, was imprisoned in Fernandina's Old Jail. . He was convicted of murder, rape, and robbery, among other crimes, and was sentenced to hang. Because of his viciousness, a huge crowd gathered to see justice done. The night before the hanging, however, Aury tried to cheat his victims of their revenge. He slit his own throat. A surgeon was called in to stitch him up enough to keep him alive to execute. On the next morning, the jailers buttoned up his collar and led him out to the gallows behind the jail. When the trap dropped, his stitches ripped open, nearly decapitating him. His blood splashed out over the crowd. Rumors say you can still hear the old scoundrel moaning behind the jail where the gallows used to be. Some people have even claimed to see his ghost stalking the area with his open throat spewing blood.

The Old Jail is one of the best places to start your tour of Fernandina at the Amelia Island Museum of History. It is the only spoken-history museum in Florida. More than 100 volunteer guides give details of the island's past at the

Finding Florida's Phantoms

museum and on walking tours of the historic district. The Historic Society also sponsors a Ghost Tour that will give you a glimpse of what the area's early days were like as well as acquaint you with many of the island's phantoms.

The best known of the local ghosts is "Uncle Charlie." He hangs out at the Palace Solon. The Palace is Florida's oldest saloon that is still operating in its original location. It was reported to be the last bar in the entire country to close for prohibition. During the hiatus, it served ice cream instead of its famous Pirate's Punch. Charlie lived in a room in the saloon and died there in 1960. His spirit is still believed to be taking care of customers. Many have glimpsed him in the mirrors behind the huge mahogany bar. In the late 1980's, it was the haunt of America's wealthiest, such as the Vanderbilt's, Dupont's and Carnegie's. Although damaged by a fire a few years ago, it has been restored to its original condition and you can still grab a sandwich and a drink or just belly up to the bar and watch for Uncle Charlie to appear.

Fernandina is filled with grand old homes, some of them still housing the presence of their original owners. One is the Eppes House on Ash Street and 10th Street. It was built around 1885 and was the home of T. J. and Celeste Eppes. Celeste was a raven-haired beauty who desired attention at all costs. Once, just to make her husband jealous, she lied and told him a family friend, Maj. Ferdinand Suhrer, was making inappropriate advances to her. She succeeded beyond her expectations and was horrified to learn that her enraged husband had shot and killed the innocent Major. The guilt must have eaten away at Celeste for years. When she and her newborn child died during childbirth, they were buried in the St. Peter's Episcopal Church graveyard nearby. But she could not rest in peace with the blood of an innocent man on her hands. She still roams her former home trying to make amends.

A 20th century owner of the Eppes House reported seeing a woman with flowing raven hair that now had a white streak in it. The apparition spoke to the woman and told her the white streak was caused by the guilt she felt for causing the death of an innocent man.

There were three historic houses built for the Thompson family in Fernandina in the late 1800's. The first of the Thompson Houses was built around 1872 for the prominent local family. It was the home of the most prominent family member, William Naylor Thompson, who was a state senator.

The Lucy Cottage was built around 1877 for his sister, Miss Lucy O. Thompson. It still remains in the Thompson family.

The last of the Thompson houses was built in 1882 for the senator's brother, Pratt Thompson. It was the city's first brick residence. His wife, "Miss Nettie," loved the old home. In fact, she is still there. Called "a tease, not a terror," she still rattles the beds and rearranges the items on the dressers in what she still considers "her home."

One of Fernandina's oldest phantoms may be the ghost of a young girl who was accused of practicing witchcraft. She was hanged in the 1600's but her spirit still guards her grave. Legends say that if you approach her grave, you will feel the ground shaking. Other times you are allowed to approach but a part of her leaves with you. You will dream of her for two nights then, if you return to the gravesite, you will actually see her. Want to check for yourself? The grave of the girl is located on the narrow path just across from Fernandina Beach High School.

One landmark that has stood the test of time well on Amelia is the lighthouse. Peeping above the trees, Florida's northernmost lighthouse has a strange history. In 1820, it began its life as Georgia's southernmost light on the southern tip of Cumberland Island. Then, in 1837, it was dismantled and moved to its present location.

Today, it is still in good shape and can be seen from the street but is no longer open to the public. As in many lighthouses, it has its tragic ghost story. It is said to be haunted by the spirit of a former keeper and his young bride. The young woman died tragically and the grief stricken keeper killed himself at the top of the lighthouse. Visitors have experienced putrid smells inside the lighthouse. One of the doors is always found unlocked even though caretakers are careful to lock it when they leave. A radio will mysteriously come on at night for no reason.

Another ghost who reportedly inhabits the old lighthouse is Amos Latham, the first keeper, who died 1842

On the coast looking towards Georgia's Cumberland Island, Fort Clinch stands as a silent sentry, a witness to American history's greatest tragedy. It was started in 1847 by the federal government and the construction continued during the Civil War. In 1961, it was taken over by the Confederates who later withdrew by order of General Lee in 1862.

Of course, it was promptly occupied by the Federal troops. During the skirmishing between the two sides, several Union soldiers were killed.

After the Civil War, it was reduced to an almost standby position, only to be briefly reactivated in 1898 for several months during the Spanish-American War. Today, it is a state park. Its remarkable state of preservation lends itself well to the reenactments conducted there regularly.

Among the Union soldiers killed at the fort was one man who promised his wife in a letter that he would not die until they were together again. He is believed to be one of the soldiers who haunt the fort today. Re-enactors at the fort often see a ghost in the courtyard who seems to be looking for someone. Many of his comrades have also been spotted.

One soldier appears in a window and has been seen by many people. He is in Yankee uniform and appears to be glowing.

Many other people have spotted a woman dressed in white, possibly a nurse. There are also those who have heard the cries of a ghostly baby. During the depression, homeless people lived in the tunnels of the fort. It is said that the ghost baby is one of homeless people who died in the cold damp conditions. There are stories that a female spirit is often spotted searching for her baby. Could this be the same crying baby ghost?

Along with all the sightings, there have been many reports of mysterious footsteps and jangling keys in the night.

When you visit Fernandina, you may want to stay at the Bailey House Bed and Breakfast. There is a ghost story attached to this magnificent Queen Ann Style Victorian.

Katherine MacDonell was born in 1874 on Amelia Island. When she was thirteen, she saw a picture of a beautiful home in a magazine and was so enthralled

Finding Florida's Phantoms

by its graceful lines and ornate gingerbread that she cut it out and told all her family and friends it was her "dream home."

A few years later, the teenaged Kate met a charming older man, Effingham W. Bailey, who was a steamship agent from Charleston, South Carolina stationed in Fernandina Beach. He was smitten and when his young fiancée showed him the picture, he promised to build it for her when they were married as soon as she was eighteen.

He kept his word and the home still stands today in all its magnificent glory. Miss Kate was a determined woman. A story is told about her run in with the authorities.

At one time, the city decided to cut down a giant, ancient, live oak tree on Ash Street, near her home. Miss Kate informed the city manager that no one had better "dare put an axe to that tree." She sat on her porch with a shotgun to protect her tree while the workers paved the street. The oak is still there and some say Mrs. Kate's ghost is still guarding that tree from her porch.

Since Amelia Island was once "the place to visit" for wealthy northern travelers before Henry Flagler's new railroad lured them father South, it had many lodgings in the 1900's. The oldest of these, perhaps the oldest hotel in Florida, is the Florida House. It is still operating as a bed and breakfast but has been vastly remodeled since the days when David Yulee built his small Vernacular "Cracker" style house in 1857 to accommodate travelers on his planned railroad from Fernandina to Cedar Key. This was to be the first cross-state railroad between the most important Florida ports on each coast.

Over the years, the hotel has been improved to create a lovely inn that still reflects the heritage of Fernandina Beach.

After almost a century, Amelia Island had been rediscovered by visitors from the North. The construction of Amelia Island Plantation once more brings the richest and the most prominent visitors back to the island.

The locals know they have had the "good life" here all along whether anyone else "discovers" it or not.

Contacts:

Amelia Island Museum of History
233 S. 3rd Street;
(904) 261-7378

Bailey House B and B
28 South 7th Street
Amelia Island, FL 32034
Toll Free: (800) 251-5390
Voice: (904) 261-5390
Facsimile: (904) 321-0103
Email: relax@bailey-house.com
www.bailey-house.com/

Florida House Inn
20 South 3rd Street
Amelia Island, Florida 32034
Reservations & Information: (800) 258-3301
To Reach a Guest: (904) 261-3300
www.floridahouseinn.com
innkeepers@floridahouseinn.com

Amelia Island Plantation
P.O. Box 3000
Amelia Island, FL 32035-3000
(888) 261-6161 Reservations
(904) 261-6161 Local and all other calls
http://www.aipfl.com/

Amelia Island State Park
12157 Heckscher Dr.
904-251-2320

Palace Saloon
117 Centre St
Fernandina Beach, FL 32034
(904) 261-6320

Jacksonville and the Beaches

Jacksonville has long been described as the hard-working brother in a family of playboys. It is shedding that image fast. More and more people are discovering the attractions that this underrated city has to offer, miles of sandy beaches, historically significant sites, ecological areas, cruises, sports, unique shopping, art galleries and of course ghosts tours.

The heart of Jacksonville is located in its downtown area. Starting from The Landing, a festival marketplace on the river with shops, eateries and entertainment, you are minutes from most of the historically significant old buildings. Many of these are ghost-infested. You can drive but parking is sometimes difficult. Your best choices are the Skyway and the trolley lines. There are four trolley lines and they are free. The Skyway is only thirty-five cents, even less if you are elderly or disabled.

One of Jacksonville's most significant downtown structures is the Florida Theatre. It originally opened on April 8, 1927. It provided early movies and vaudeville acts. Then there were fifteen lavish movie theaters. Today, it is the city's last remaining example of 1920's style movie palace.

But it has something more than interesting architecture. It still has one of the original technicians from the 1920's. He's dead, of course, but that doesn't stop Doc Crowther from continuing to monitor the theater's activities and look out for the current maintenance man.

Earliest reports of Doc began with some of the cleaning people who saw "something" in the projection booth many years ago. Since then he has been observed by many of the theatergoers and employees. He is usually found in the balcony. Lights go off and on without the benefit of human activity. The theater's ghost became so well known that a local television station did a special on him several years ago. They brought in psychic, Jill Cook-Richards, to investigate. Ms. Cook-Richards definitely confirmed a presence there. She actually saw him. She reported, that he wanted to be called "J" for "Joy" in the future

The ghost has never been harmful and has instead been helpful on at least one occasion. Saundra Floyd, director of rental operations, was leading a tour of schoolchildren through the theater. Some of them became mischievous and began playing with the projectors.

Ms. Floyd told them that the ghost does not want them to do that and he will become upset and turn the light off if they continued. The children were unconvinced, until the lights actually did go out in that area. The children immediately joined the group and began to behave. The amazed teacher asked, "How did you do that?"

She was even more amazed when she learned that Ms. Floyd had not turned the lights out at all.

The theater is not the only haunted building downtown. 1887 Building, 501 West Bay Street, is now the offices of Sullivan and Associates, maritime lawyers and two other legal related businesses. It was originally the El Modelo Cigar Factory. After the factory shut down, it became a saloon and boarding house. It was while it was in this incarnation that the incident that triggered the haunting occurred.

In 1907, a Spanish-American War veteran was murdered by a blast to his chest fired from a sawed-off shotgun as he entered the front door of the bar. The door was located in the southeast corner of the building and you can feel a cold spot in that place. Workers often refuse to work alone in that part of the building at night. The building is on the National Resister of Historic Places.

Two other Bay Street buildings, the Blackstone Building, 233 E. Bay Street, and the Churchwell Building, 301-313 East Bay Street, also have resident spirits. Blackstone's spirit is said to mostly hang around suite 711. The Churchwell Building boasts a young female spirit wearing a copper colored dress looking out the window.

The residence of Captain W. J. King also harbors a spirit. Captain King was a St. Johns River bar pilot. This one has been investigated and confirmed by Duke University Parapsychology Department.

It's not only the buildings in Jacksonville that have unearthly residents. Stories abound of a haunting presence on the Dames Point Bridge. Some report that she is an African American woman who either fell or jumped to her death from the bridge. Others say it was a Caucasian woman.

Restaurants often have their own ghosts. The Stonewood Grill located in Southside near Baymeadows and San Jose has a whopper and I don't mean a burger.

The disturbances began almost as soon as it opened three years ago. Lee Boyer, the operating partner and his staff began hearing noises. The fires came on under pans that had been turned off.

One night the night manager had turned off all the burners and went outside. He heard a noise and rushed back in to find the burners turned back on. If that wasn't enough to spook him, when he looked back outside, a sign that had previously been lying on the ground was now standing on its edge with the posts sticking up in the air. Nothing was holding it up. It just stood there.

The site has never been a cemetery and no one had died violently there to Boyer's knowledge. However, the place next door where Walgreen's is today, used to be a rough and rowdy bar called Motorboat Mel's. Several people got

Finding Florida's Phantoms

knifed there and the owner committed suicide in the building. Perhaps some of those wild spirits are still looking for a little excitement.

People expect the residents of a cemetery to stay put but not so in some of Jacksonville's old cemeteries. Old City Cemetery near Springfield has at least two wraiths that have been seen through the years. One is of a murdered Black woman who is buried near the rear of the cemetery.

The other was the subject of a sensational "unsolved" crime. Louise Gato was a wealthy and beautiful nineteen-year-old woman. She was shot fatally as she entered her parent's home in Springfield on April 20, 1897.

She regained consciousness long enough to sign an affidavit that the assailant was a former boy friend, Edward George Pitzer.

Pitzer denied the charges and claimed he was visiting another woman at the time of the attack. A strange side story to the murder was that the detective investigating the case, William Gruber, was killed while investigating another case. He was found lying in the bushes with his scull crushed. A woman's blue belt and small white handkerchief were found nearby.

The defense succeeded in having the signed statement thrown out as evidence. They claimed Miss Gato was not capable of making that determination.

Were the two killings related? No one ever found out. Both murders remain unsolved.

But Louise is still seeking justice. She was unable to have justice carried out so she still walks the old cemetery to remind people of her unavenged murder.

Evergreen Cemetery, 4535 North Main Street, is Jacksonville's oldest operating cemetery. It covers about seventy acres and has about 70,000 burial sites. It was established in 1881 and was the "in" place to be buried in the early days of the city. Isaiah D. Hart, Jacksonville's founder, is there as are politicians, business leaders, paupers and prostitutes, a Confederate General, the rich and famous, as well as the poor and downtrodden. Some of those who are not resting in peace include a Woman in Violet, a man in Confederate uniform and the spirit of a woman who is always seen near the "Ugly Angel" Tombstone.

One of Jacksonville's most known tales is that of the Greenbriar Road Light. Drivers on this road near the St. Johns County line have frequently seen what appears to be a single headlight behind them in the rearview mirror. It will follow cars for miles but is not really there. The story is that a motorcyclist was killed in an accident. His head was severed from his body. The light is believed to be that headless cyclist hunting his missing appendage.

While Jacksonville proper has many amenities, it is the beach with its sun and surf that attracts many visitors and it certainly has its share of hauntings.

The Casa Marina was built in 1925, the oldest inn in Jacksonville Beach. Through all the years, it still retains its Gilded Era charm. Perhaps it retains a few of its early inhabitants as well. The newspapers of the day touted it as the safest place to stay since they had a state of the art fire sprinkler system. The building was the first fireproof building on the beach. The then 60-room hotel offered a living room filled with wicker furniture where their wealthy and powerful guests could relax, dine and dance the night away. Most of the rooms had an unobstructed ocean view. The Spanish Mediterranean style with its terra-cotta tile roof was reminiscent of many of Hollywood's most palatial homes.

When World War 11 struck, it was transformed into military housing. After the war, it went through various hands and degenerated from apartments into a boarded up derelict.

From 1987 to 1991, it remained forsaken. Then new owners, Allan and Mary Lou Brown, began renovating it back to its original splendor. They reopened it in April 2001. In August 2002, the present owner took it over and pledged to remain faithful to the splendid building's early purpose.

When you dine in its restaurant today, you will be served by a cheerful staff. The food will be the freshest available. Chef Aaron Bean will prepare it in an innovating and tempting way. You can order over 44 wines by the glass or bottle. You can choose mixed drinks crafted to perfection by bar manager, Mark Vandeloo.

The menu is varied. Items like Seafood Crepes, Fried Goat Cheese Salad or Flounder Spanaki, (a flounder filet rolled around spinach, feta and parmesan cheese baked in a fylo pastry and topped with Dijon cream) are some of the more exotic fare served at the Casa Marina. If you are more of a conservative, you will be ecstatic over their Roasted Chicken or Grilled Rack of Lamb. For lunch, you can choose a lighter fare like soup, salad or sandwiches.

However, while your waiter serves your meal, keep a sharp lookout for another shadowy figure also bearing trays of food. You may catch a glimpse of a waiter from bygone times. The story goes that in the inn's heyday, formally dressed black waiters tended to the lustrous patrons' needs.

One of these young men, perhaps hurrying to serve exacting customers, fell through one of the dinning room's tall floor level windows and died on the pavement below. His spirit is believed to roam the kitchen and dining areas of the Casa Marina to this day. One restaurant employee who wishes to remain anonymous also claims that there is another spirit in the Casa Marina, a woman who was murdered in the building by her husband. This person states that there is hardly any member of the staff who has not experienced "something strange." She even said that one housekeeper was actually touched by the phantom and almost went into hysterics.

Another landmark Beach restaurant that reopened recently was the Homestead Restaurant.

Kathy and Malcolm Marvin, and their partner and general manager Teresa Pratt, are no stranger to the restaurant or its legend. Kathy's father, Preben Johansen, originally purchased the business in 1962 from Alpha O. Paynter shortly before her death.

Alpha was the one who originally saw the potential in a restaurant at this site. She had inherited the two-story, circa 1934 pine log house from a man she came here to nurse. For a time she ran an adoption and foster home in it and then converted it into a restaurant in the 1940's. She lived in one part and used the rest to serve her customers, travelers along the newly constructed Beach Blvd. She probably feels she has the last laugh. She started the business and then sold it but has gone right on hanging around. She must feel right at home since most of the traditional features of the original building are still intact such as the massive limestone fireplace, the log walls, pine flooring and exposed ceiling joists.

Finding Florida's Phantoms

I spoke to Kenny Harrell, prep cook at the Homestead. He is a large man who has traveled around the country a bit. He formerly worked in a well-known restaurant in New Orleans and is not the type of person who would scare easily. Still, he said, "I'm a little bit leery of the ghosts in the Homestead. When I come in in the morning to begin preparations for the evening dining, Nina (Nina Marvin, the owner's daughter) comes in first, opens up and puts on some lights before I come in. I then go straight to the kitchen and put the radio on loud. That way I can focus on the music and not hear anything else that I might not want to hear."

I asked if he had ever heard "anything he didn't want to" and he replied he had. "When I was just a teenager and played football, some of us guys would come in here then but when we heard strange noises coming from upstairs, we would all run out"

"What about now when you are working. Ever see or hear anything?" I asked.

He replied, "Yes often I hear noises, doors slamming and sounds from the office upstairs when no one is there. That's where she died, the old lady that used to live here. Scott (head chef Scott Jinks) is scared to be in here by himself, too"

When I spoke to Nina Marvin, she said she had never personally seen anything but many of the customers had reported seeing Alpha Paynter, "Often by the fireplace in the back dining room."

A hammock just inside the navy base has Pompeii. Dwight Wilson, of the historic society, told me that both his wife and father-in-law saw Pompeii. Many of the old timers have seen or heard strange things in the hammock.

Perhaps the high ground of a hammock with its moss-draped oaks is natural setting for a ghost. If you cross the river on the Mayport Ferry, a delightful experience in its own right, and drive north on A1A (Heckscher Drive), you will cross a series of barrier islands.

One of the area's magnificent old plantations is the Kingsley Plantation. It has a terrifying phantom, Old Red Eyes. He is believed to be the evil spirit of a slave who raped and murdered two young girls. Eventually he was caught and hanged from a huge oak tree near the driveway. He is most often seen as a blazing pair of red eyes in your rear view mirror as you drive away from the plantation at night. The plantation was built by Zephaniah Kingsley who married Anna Madgigaine Jai Kingsley, an African woman who was one of his slaves whom he had freed,

After his death, Anna managed the plantation. During the Civil War, she had to flee because of her ardent Unionist sentiments. The plantation grew Sea Island cotton and is the oldest remaining plantation house left in Florida. There are also reports of a man and woman seen at the plantation and at the site of some tabby ruins before you reach the plantation entrance. Perhaps they are Zephaniah and his beloved Anna.

If you continue on north, you will come to Little Talbot and Big Talbot Islands. Both have state parks on them and are great places for bird watching or just strolling the beaches. Another interesting spot to visit is BEAKS on Big Talbot Island. It is a bird and wildlife rehabilitation sanctuary that welcomes visitors. You might ask the owners to tell you a few of their favorite ghost stories about the island.

There are many ghosts on this island. The entire island once belonged to the Christopher and Houston families. Spicer Christopher acquired the island in 1783 and raised cotton, indigo, horses and cattle. John Houston, called "Big John," married Spicer's daughter, Elizabeth Susannah Christopher, combining the two families into one even wealthier one.

When Elizabeth died, "Big John" married a relative of his first wife named Mary Braddock Greenwood. Many of these families intermarried and many of them are buried in the cemetery now called just the Houston Cemetery. John McQueen, who was immortalized in Eugenia Price's *Don Juan McQueen*, also lived in the area for a time. The cemetery is reportedly haunted by the planters as well as their slaves.

To reach the cemetery, go to the old rest area on the left just a short way after you reach the island, then go to Houston Road about 200 yards north of the rest area on the left. Follow Houston Road about a mile and a half and you will come to the cemetery. People have heard the sound of dogs barking here and tape-recorded it. But when the tape is played back, the barking isn't on the tape, just the normal voices of the group. Unexplained mists and cold spots also occur here. Photographs often show orbs. The cemetery is very old and some of the crypts are open creating an eerie atmosphere.

The island also had a Timcuan burial site near the same area. It is down a trail that begins about 300 yards north of the rest area on the right. Here you may hear moaning and again spot orbs. The temperature is always many degrees colder than the surrounding area.

Farther north on the island is an area called "The Bluffs." People camping or hiking in there have sensed a feeling of evil especially at night. If you go there, it is wise to not go alone. Phenomena reported include apparitions, barking as of large dogs, and strange voices.

After all this mystery and unexplained happenings, it may be nice to just lie on the beach and soak up the sun. Jacksonville Beach will soon have a new pier to accommodate this. Work is well underway. The pier will be 20 feet wide and extend 1,300 feet with a large enclosed deck on the end.

Contacts:

Visitor Information Department
(800)-733-2668, Ext. 10
(904)798-9111, Ext. 10
visitorinfo@jaxcvb.com

Jacksonville Haunted History Tours
From Jacksonville Landing
(904) 276-2098
http://jhht.cjb.net/

Finding Florida's Phantoms

Fort Caroline National Memorial
12713 Fort Caroline Road
Jacksonville, FL 32225
(904) 641-7155
(904) 641-3798 fax

Budweiser Brewery Tour
111 Busch Dr.
Jacksonville, FL 32218
904-751-8116
904-751-8095 fax
www.budweisertours.com

Jacksonville Princess
1201 Riverplace Boulevard
Jacksonville, FL 32207
(904) 398-8800 Ext. 4110
(904)396-8844 fax

Jacksonville Zoological Gardens
8605 Zoo Parkway
Jacksonville, FL 32218
904-757-4463
904-757-4315 fax
www.jaxzoo.org

Museum of Science and History (MOSH)
1025 Museum Circle
Jacksonville, FL 32207
904-396-MOSH
904-396-5799 fax

Ritz Theatre & La Villa Museum
829 N. Davis Street
Jacksonville, FL 32202
904-632-5555
904-632-5553 fax

River Cruises, Inc.
Wharfside Way
Jacksonville, FL 32207
904-396-2333
1800-711-3470 ext.7304 toll-free
904-396-5599 fax
www.rivercruise.com

SunCruz Casino
4378 Ocean Street
Atlantic Beach, FL 32233
904-322-9600
904-756-1342 fax

Talbot Islands State Parks
12157 Heckscher Drive
Jacksonville, FL 32226
904-251-2320
904-251-2325 fax

Timcuan Preserve/Kingsley Plantation
11676 Palmetto Avenue
Jacksonville, FL 32226
(904) 251-3537
(904) 251-3577 fax

B.E.A.K.S.
12084 Houston Avenue
Big Talbot Island, Florida 32226
(904) 251-BIRD
Open Tuesday through Sunday
12 noon until 4 pm

Transportation
Trollys
http://jtaonthemove.com/service/trol/
Skyway
http://jtaonthemove.com/service/sky/map/

Florida Theater
128-134 E. Forsyth St.
Jacksonville, Florida

Finding Florida's Phantoms

St. Augustine

When the Pilgrims finally landed at Plymouth Rock in 1620, St. Augustine was already a thriving settlement. It had a fort, a church, a hospital, shops and over 100 houses. It has accumulated ghost tales for over four and a half centuries.

Fort Matanzas - the back door to St. Augustine! Just 14 miles south of the nation's oldest city, where the Matanzas River touches the Atlantic, is the windswept estuary where the Spanish heritage of Florida was indelibly sealed in the blood of 245 murdered French prisoners. Here, in 1565, the inlet earned its name - Matanzas, Spanish for slaughter.

With such a bloody beginning, is it any wonder that the nation's oldest city is besieged with restless spirits?

The drama that ended on this mosquito-infested inlet that October day more than four centuries ago revolves around two reckless European explorers, Pedro Menendez de Aviles and Jean Ribault.

Pedro Menendez was a younger son of a minor Spanish nobleman. He had served his king since he was 15. His fortunes had risen and fallen frequently. They were at a very low ebb in early 1565. He and his brother had been imprisoned by the Casa de Contratocion, the governing body for the American trade. As if this was not bad enough, he received word that his only son Juan had been lost in a shipwreck in the Caribbean.

He finally was able to appear before King Phillip and state his case. The King was sympathetic and not only reinstated Menendez as Captain General, but named him Governor of Florida and gave him an important injunction; explore and colonize the new land of Florida for Spain and drive out any settlers of other nations.

Meanwhile in France, Jean Ribault received his orders from Gaspard de Coligny, Admiral of France. Protect the French colony of Fort Caroline in Florida. Do not let Menendez encroach on it. Ribault was a veteran seaman who had made at least one other voyage to the New World. He was given several fast vessels and reinforcements. He hurriedly set sail for Fort Caroline. He and Menendez were both able tacticians and wily fighters.

He was a Huguenot, as were most of the French colonists. France was a country torn by war with Spain and civil strife between the Catholic majority and the Huguenot minority.

Both men arrived in Florida on August 28th. Ribault sailed directly to the sod and timber Fort Caroline on the St. Johns River near what is now Jacksonville.

Menendez landed near Cape Canaveral. He turned north and began seeking the French. On September 3rd, Menendez found a place with a good harbor. He called this place San Augustine. On September 5th, the two men made the first contact, Menendez on his "San Pelayo" and Ribault on his flagship "Trinity." A few shots were fired and the French slipped away. The Spaniards gave chase but were outdistanced quickly. Menendez returned to the place he had decided to establish his colony and on September 8th, he officially founded the colony of San Augustine. He was located about 38 miles south of Fort Caroline. Realizing the vulnerability of his big galleons that could not come across the shallow bar in the harbor, Menendez sent them back to Santo Domingo on September 10th.

Ribault sailed in pursuit of the two vessels. Fate intervened in form of a typical Florida hurricane blowing the French fleet before it with a vengeance. Menendez, realizing that the storm would prevent Ribault's return to Fort Caroline in time, marched his men overland through swamps and swollen streams in the torrential downpour to Fort Caroline. He captured it without the loss of a single Spaniard. Of the 240 Frenchmen, they killed 132. A few escaped but the victory was overwhelming. Menendez returned to San Augustine, believing that if Ribault had survived the storm, he would attack the settlement while the main body of soldiers were away.

Meanwhile, weary and waterlogged, two separate groups of shipwrecked Frenchmen were slowly making their way back towards Fort Caroline. When Menendez heard this, he began moving south with between 50 and 70 men until he reached the south end of Anastasia Island. There, at a small inlet, he encountered the first contingent of 126 Frenchmen. Already dispirited by the shipwreck and the weather, they surrendered to him. The prisoners were fed and bound. They were then led down the beach a little ways and, with the exception of 15 Catholics, all were killed. On October 12th, Ribault and 350 remaining Frenchmen arrived at the inlet. Menendez ordered him to surrender. About half of the Frenchmen decided to take to the woods rather than trust Menendez to show mercy. The remaining 150 surrendered. All but 16 were slaughtered in the already bloody marsh. France had forever lost her chance in Florida and the population of New World ghosts was dramatically increased. Many people have claimed to see apparitions of bloody French soldiers plodding in the marsh.

Today, this area is administered by the National Park Service. It is called Fort Matanzas National Monument in honor of the fort the Spanish built there in 1742. The fort is built of native coquina to replace the earlier wooden watchtower they constructed to protect them from English invasion. It is small but easily defended since it is located on tiny Rattlesnake Island and is accessible only by water. During its occupation, it usually housed 7 to 10 enlisted men and one junior officer. It then housed five cannons. The two remaining cannons are the

Finding Florida's Phantoms

original ones left when the Spanish abandoned the fort after the United States acquired Florida in 1821. Today, a permanent stairway replaces the wooden ladder used by the soldiers in the daytime and drawn up every night. A shuttle ferry runs between the fort and the Anastasia Island portion of the park from 9 to 5 daily except Christmas.

The park consists of 298 acres including both Rattlesnake Island and part of Anastasia Island. The Anastasia side houses a visitor center with a small museum and a boardwalk nature trail. The trail winds through scrub and woodland that appear untouched since those fateful days in 1565. It abounds with birds and small wildlife. At places, patches of colorful wild flowers decorate the sandy soil. All that remains today of the slaughter there is a small wooden sign commemorating the spot where it occurred. The boardwalk breaks through the palmetto at the river's edge where you can see both the fort and the inlet to ocean. Today, small motor boats and modern sailboats ply the waters that were once the domain of the heavy Spanish Galleons.

The park is free and open daily except Christmas. It also has a picnic area and an ocean beach access. Only a small portion of The First Coast's many tourists finds their way here. Those who do are well rewarded. They get a chance to see for themselves a turning point in the beginnings of European culture in the New World. As is true with many National Monuments, the federal government does not encourage "ghost stories" but, after you learn the history, would you care to spend the night here? Whatever the reason, the park is closed to visitors after dark but even as twilight shadows lengthen, you cannot help but feel the stirring of these murdered souls. Many must still remain here.

In spite of their ruthless battle practices, the Spanish were a very religious people so one of the first things they did upon landing in St. Augustine was hear Mass offered by the ship's chaplain, Father Lopez.

This Mass was celebrated at the site of the Great Cross on the ground of The Mission de Nombre de Dios. The cross was erected in 1965 to commemorate the mission's 400th anniversary. The stainless steel cross-towers 208 feet and can be seen for miles out to sea at night.

At the very front of the grounds, you will see the Prince of Peace Church. It is the newest of the shrines and altars on this ancient site. Built in 1965, it commemorates 400 years of the Catholic faith in the New World and was dedicated to world peace. On December 1, 2002, a strange event occurred at the church. At around 1 p.m., Jill Valley, her mother-in-law and her two children were decorating the altar. Jill was leaning on a pew when she heard a sound "like tiny pebbles dropping on the pew." Then the sound accelerated "like a truckload of sand being dumped."

Suddenly tiles from the floor began flying into the air, some as high as eye level. The Valley's fled the scene as if pursued by demons. Jill Valley stated, "It was the weirdest thing that any one of us had ever seen."

Explanations of why the phenomena occurred ran the gauntlet from scientific to superstition. None ever really made sense. Eric Johnson, the director of the Nombre de Dios Mission, speculated that it could have been cold induced contractions of the church's coquina walls or concrete floor. Yet, he admitted there was no cracking in the walls or windows, just the floor tiles.

The elder Mrs. Valley speculated that it might have been because she was Presbyterian. Not too likely that whatever caused it cared what denomination the witnesses were.

Another explanation offered and just as quickly refuted is that it was a sinkhole. However, sinkholes would have caused things to sonic. In this case, the tiles flew upward.

Mr. Johnson was quick to point out that he wasn't blaming anything supernatural. It had to be something that could be explained by science and physics. Perhaps.

When the same sort of thing happened in two properties managed by Tom Rivers, a local realtor, he had a different explanation. "It's a ghost that throws things around," he said. "This one likes to move floors."

Contractors and engineers called in in each of the three cases could find on evidence of any problems with the structures. So maybe Tom Rivers is right about his "Floor Poltergeist."

Some of the real estate in St. Augustine has been accumulating psychic energy for centuries. The oldest house in the city is the González-Alvarez House. A Spanish soldier, Tomás González, built it for his family around 1702. Church records document that one of the children died there in 1727. Perhaps it is the child that haunts the home. Perhaps it is a spirit that stayed there at a later time. No one knows for sure but many people will agree, "something" outside the normal is there.

This building is one of the most studied homes in America because it is so well documented. A national historic landmark, the house has a history of continuous occupancy from its construction on into the twentieth century. It is one of the favorite house-museums in St. Augustine and a must see for anyone who was a fan of Eugenia Price who immortalized it in her novel, *Maria*.

As Spain secured its hold on this part of the New World, a main fort guarding the colony became necessary. The Queen of Spain decreed the building of Castillo de San Marcos. This was in 1672. At that time, the Spanish had captured a young English pirate named Andrew Ranson. Since pirates had sacked and burned the city and plundered the supply shops, feeling ran high about the penalty that should be exacted. Ranson was sentenced to be garroted. The executioner, not having an official garrote available, used a makeshift one. He drilled a hole at neck height in a straight palm tree. On the day of the execution, the pirate was marched to the tree, a rope inserted through the hole and encircling his neck. Behind the tree, the executioner placed a stick through the loop of the makeshift noose and began to turn it. In preparation for death, Andrew took out a rosary from his pocket and began to pray. The priest in the audience noted the rosary and wondered what a Protestant Englishman was doing praying a Catholic Rosary. No sooner had the pirate begun his prayer, than the stick used to twist the rope ever tighter broke. Andrew fell to the ground and the priest grabbed him and led him into the cathedral. He believed God was sparing the young man's life for a reason.

Since in those days a church was sacred ground and no one could be taken from it, Andrew was safe for the moment. He was badly rope burned, however, and needed someone to treat the sores. The priest asked a young girl in the congregation, the executioner's fourteen-year-old daughter, to tend to the prisoner.

Finding Florida's Phantoms

Within a short time, the girl and the pirate were in love, to her father's shame. He decided to find out more about the pirate who had captured his daughter's heart.

He discovered that Andrew Ranson had been a stonemason before seeking a life on the high seas. Since the city needed a good stonecutter to build the proposed fort and since his daughter was adamant about her love for the pirate, the executioner struck a deal for the young man. He would gain a pardon for him and all his crew if they would stay and build the fort. If he did a good job of it and wanted to remain, he would give him his daughter's hand.

Obviously, Andrew Ranson did a wonderful job. The fort's unique building material, coquina, a type of shell-stone quarried from Anastasia Island, absorbed cannon blast rather than crumbling. Perhaps it is for this reason that the fort had never been conquered. It changed hands may times but always by treaty. Although it belonged to the British, the United States and the Confederacy during the Civil War, it is the original Spanish construction and influence that remains strongest. But people in the area are reminded of its English connection by the many "Ranson's" still in the area. Yes, the pirate did remain here and marry the executioner's daughter.

Perhaps some other Spanish influences lurk around the fort as well. The old fort has rumors of restless spirits from the days of Florida's Spanish domination who still roam its dank tunnels to this day. One tale of illicit love and jealous rage may explain the rumors of a strange glow and a perfume smell within the walls of the fort. Colonel Garcia Marti had a beautiful young wife. Perhaps she was neglected as the colonel went about his duties or maybe she just grew bored in this tiny colonial town. Whatever the reason, she began a clandestine affair with her husband's assistant, Captain Manuel Abela. The story goes that the colonel found out and murdered both of them, tossing the bodies into a shallow grave in one of the deepest dungeons. Later, bones of man and woman were found in the dungeon. Rumors of a perfume smell and an eerie glow in the area persist.

The fort protected the fledgling town and allowed it to prosper. When you visit today and wander down St. George St., much of the original colony is preserved or recreated. The old Spanish village with its living history re-creation of what life was like in the 1600 and 1700's is a wonderful place to be transported to that era. The oldest schoolhouse is still open to visitors. Many of the ghost tours begin here in the oldest city's historic quarter area. And with good reason. The Old Spanish Bakery is a great place to sample a pastry but if you are lucky, you may catch a glimpse of the mysterious spirit who still hangs her ghostly garment in the courtyard.

St Augustine transferred into British hands in 1763. During the transfer, many families were uprooted. The customs and religions of the two countries were too far apart for many of the Spanish families to remain under British domination. One case gave rise to a restless spirit who still remains in her ancient home.

The home was built in 1750, and was the dwelling place of the DePorras family. There were nine children in the family and the youngest was a fiery beauty named Catalina.

Kathleen Walls

The DePorres family departed for Cuba when the colony was ceded to England. She grew into womanhood and married while in Cuba but she always yearned for her childhood home.

Her chance came when the Spanish returned to Florida in 1783. She must have been a headstrong woman because she persuaded both her husband and the new Spanish governor that this home on 46 Avenida Menendez was where she belonged. Indeed, she felt so at home there she still resides on the property.

The original home was burned in 1877 but Catalina must still have been working her will. It was rebuilt to resemble the original home.

It has been a series of restaurants in modern times. Once it was named in her honor, Catalina's Gardens. Today it is Harry's Seafood Bar and Grill. But Catalina is still throwing her weight around.

Bill Boyd, a manager at Harry's, recounts his experience with Catalina.

He was putting up curtains in the old part of the building. He felt as if someone was in the room but no one was there. After he got the curtains up, he turned to gather up the tools and leave. The curtains, rod and all, were yanked off the wall and tossed across the room. Perhaps Catalina did not like the color or style.

Catalina seems to have been joined by a mysterious man in black. While Catalina is seen and felt most frequently in the upstairs part, the man dressed in black from head to foot and sporting an old-fashioned black hat is seen downstairs, often near the fireplace. He will stare at women diners. If they complain to the management, the man will disappear before the manager can arrive on the scene.

Perhaps it is the man who caused the disturbance that another manager, Linda, experienced with the burglar alarm going off repeatedly. When the police arrived, no one was there and there was no sign of a break in. Finally, when they entered the building after one of the false alarms, she and police observed the lights above the bar swinging for no apparent reason.

Catalina's home is not the only old Spanish building having a permanent resident related to the brief period the British dominated this part of Florida.

Just around the corner from St. Augustine's Oldest House, stands the St. Francis Inn, the city's oldest inn. It was built by Gaspar Garciaon on a lot granted to him by the King of Spain in 1791.

Now since he was a mere sergeant and would not normally have been able to afford the magnificent thick walled fortress style home, the fact that he was in charge of construction of the public buildings for the government might explain his living so far above his means. He had access to the best building materials and tools available in his day.

St Francis Inn has two permanent residents, Lily and her lover. Lily was a beautiful slave girl who worked in the home in the 1800's. A young British soldier lodged in the house. The two fell hopelessly in love. They had clandestine trysts in a room on the third floor. Today it is called Lily's room.

Since the property was built after the British occupation of the area, the affair probably took place during the ownership of Colonel Thomas Henry Dummett, since he himself was retired from Britain's Royal marines, or his daughter, Anna. She was the one who converted the family home into a lodging establishment in 1845. She raised 10 nieces and nephews in the inn, children of

Finding Florida's Phantoms

three of her deceased sisters. Since she was a staunch Confederate during the war and a slave owner, this is the most likely time frame for the doomed love affair.

The young soldier was probably one of Anna's nephews. The affair was discovered when Lily became pregnant. The family was able to end the affair but not Lily's love. Rather than live without her lover, she hanged herself in the attic room where had met. It is now named Lily's Room and one of the most popular rooms in the inn.

Many people have reported seeing Lily. They usually see her from the back. They seldom her face. She is known for playing around with the female guests' makeup and jewelry, perhaps since she had no such amenities to make herself attractive for her soldier. Guests, especially in Lily's room, often tell of being touched or gently kissed at night while in their beds. Psychics who investigated the inn found lipsticks they deliberately left on a dresser unmoved while other lipsticks from the investigators' private bags mysteriously moved to other places. They did not see Lily but recorded disturbances and sounds in "her" room. They did see a slightly built Hispanic male and an older man dressed in a tri-cornered hat. No one has any explanation for these apparitions.

Bev Lonergan, who works at the St Francis, told me of an unusual experience. She was working the front desk on the night shift. "I got off at 10:30 one night and was sitting downstairs figuring out the books. I felt the hair on the back of my neck and arms start to stand up as if I had received a fright. When I looked up there was the soldier! He was short and was wearing a bright red uniform coat with brass buttons, just leaning against the wall with his arms folded. He was looking straight at me and smiling. Then he was gone." She got out of there fast and left the books for the next day.

Bev also says she has frequently glimpsed Lily but always from the back as the phantom girl hurries away from her. She hopes that "One day Lily will trust me enough to show her face."

Another old Spanish building that has its ghostly tales is O. C. Whites.

It was constructed in 1791 by Don Miguel Ysnardy, a merchant ship owner, military official and building contractor. He also was the builder of the St. Augustine Cathedral. At one time, it was used as a hotel. In the 1800's, the home was bought by Mrs. Margaret S. Worth, the widow of Major General William J. Worth, a Revolutionary War hero.

David White now owns the building and operates it as a restaurant but he admits that the ghosts of years past are still active in the building. Kerry Sullivan worked at O. C. White's. He told of working near the bar one day and smelling a strong odor of urine and body odor. He remarked, "I mentioned to another worker, 'Somebody needs to clean around the bar. It smells awful.' The other guy replied, 'It's just the ghost.' I went back there and sniffed. The odor was gone. This happened many times while I worked there. Apparently, the original owner, an older lady, did not take too much care with personal hygiene as she got older. Folks say she still hangs around the bar." Could it be old Mrs. Worth?

Kerry also worked at Scarlett O'Hara's, another popular bar and restaurant in the old city. He had a rather unnerving experience there. As he tells it, "It was real busy one night so I decided to use the rest room on the second floor. I was just finishing buckling my pants and washing my hands when I heard the door rattle like someone wanted to get in. I reached over and unlocked the door and no one was there. It was too far to the stairs for anyone to have gotten out of sight that quickly. It really made me nervous."

The importance placed on religions in St. Augustine created another opportunity for spirits to be restless. There were two cemeteries in the old days in the city, a Huguenot and a Catholic Cemetery. Both have reported sightings of restless spirits.

Tolomoto Cemetery was the Catholic one. It was the site of the Tolomoto Indian burial ground. Shannon O'Toole, a guide on the Ghost Tour, tells of an experience there. "I was guiding a group of the graders. I had my back to the cemetery and was telling a story to the kids. They began to fidget and finally broke and ran to their bus. When we calmed them down, they all told the same story. They saw a young boy about five years old dressed in knee pants and a white linen shirt. He came up from one of the graves and drifted up into the branches of an old oak tree where he sat and made faces at the children."

She felt they must have been telling the truth because "I don't see how 30 fourth graders could have made up identical stories on the spot. Even if they sat around in class and made up what they were going to say, how could they have known the tree and the grave were going to be right where each of them described? Another guide also had a similar experience with a group of girl scouts."

Not knowing the child's name might have been the guides gave him the nickname of "Nicolas." Upon investigation, Shannon found that there had been a little boy buried there. His gravestone is a little short stone with the name "James P. Morgan" and the dates make him five years and ten days old. For that reason, she believes that must be the boy the children saw.

The cemetery also has had reports of other ghosts. A Franciscan Missionary, Father Corpa, was killed by a Native American on this spot and is said to roam here at night.

There is also a lady in black haunting the cemetery as well. She seeks Colonel Smith. She was married but fell in love with the handsome colonel at a ball given in his honor. She succumbed to a fever she contracted right after the ball. Her weeping family, according to her family tradition, carried her to the cemetery in a chair. As they approached the cemetery, a thorn from an overhanging tree pricked her cheek and blood flowed. Colonel Smith saw the cut and called out that she was alive and the family rushed her home to nurse back to health.

She lived on for another six years but never regained her health or her beauty. Then she once more fell victim to the raging fever. Again, she appeared to die. This time her husband, who had lost interest in his no longer young and beautiful wife, made sure she was not carried anywhere near the tree. She was buried in the family tomb. There are those who claim she did not die and still searchs for Colonel Joseph Smith to once more rescue her from the grave where she has lain since 1829.

Just down the block from the cemetery, the city's oldest drug store was built right on top of the grave of Chief Tolomoto. After the store was built, they tried moving the stone out of the way and all sorts of strange things happened. They put the stone back and all was quiet again. So to this day, Chief Tolomoto's grave is still marked by the stone in the old drugstore.

Finding Florida's Phantoms

Just outside of the city gates at the Huguenot Cemetery, the most sighted spirit is that of Judge Stickney. John Stickney was what was commonly called a "carpetbagger." He came to St. Augustine after the Civil War with his three daughters. He was a lawyer who was appointed judge. When he died of typhoid fever, he was buried here under a stately oak tree.

His good friend, John Long in Washington, D.C., had agreed that if anything happened to the judge, he would raise the three daughters like his own children. So after the good judge died, the girls went to live in Washington with their adoptive father. Twenty-one years later, after John Long had also died and was interred in Washington, the girls agreed it would be a good thing if their real father could be moved to lie besides their adopted one in Washington.

So they hired a gravedigger named Wells to disinter their father so that he could be moved to Washington. Gravedigger Wells finally got the coffin out of the ground. But the carriage had not arrived to pick up the body so old man Wells decided to lie down in the shadow of the big oak and take a nap while he waited.

As he slept, two intoxicated rogues who had perhaps felt the judge's justice during his lifetime spotted the body. The answer to how their next binge would be financed was solved. They forced open the judge's mouth and pried out his gold teeth.

Perhaps this is why many people have sighted the judge, dressed in a tall hat and long cape, walking bent over, as if he's looking for something. Could it be his teeth?

The judge may even have been caught on videotape during one of his late night walks. Shannon told of an encounter that she didn't even know she'd had. "A friend's brother was on my tour one night. The brother videotaped it. When the friend was watching the video, she asked her brother, 'Was anyone behind her there that night in the cemetery?' 'No,' he answered. 'There is now,' she replied. Sure enough in the background of the tape, there is a dark figure of a man in top hat and cape walking towards the visitor center. Had to be John Stickney!"

Just across from the cemetery are the City Gates. In early days of the settlement, these gates were closed at dark and nothing got them opened before dawn. One of the gatekeepers had a daughter, Elizabeth. Elizabeth's ambition was to grow up and become a gatekeeper herself. Her wish was not to be. She died in a yellow fever epidemic. However, on dark nights many people have seen a young girl wrapped in a white sheet here at the city gates waving to people entering the city. Could it be that Elizabeth has achieved in death what was denied her in life?

During the second Spanish period in St. Augustine history, had you been a sick or injured soldier you would have been treated at the Spanish Military Hospital. You can tour the museum that is part of this hospital but parts of the place are forbidden to the public. They are reserved for the departed souls of those who died in the old hospital long ago. The curator, Diana Lane, has started a ghost tour that does an after hours tour of the building.

There is a door that opens and closes by itself. It has an old time latch that must be manipulated to open. You can hear the latch open and there is no one on the other side. One of the workers actually videotaped the door opening and closing by itself.

The hospital functioned from 1784 to 1821 and was built on the first Spanish period's graveyard in what had been an Indian burial ground when the settlers arrived. When the city installed new sewer lines several years ago, they found both Spanish bones and Native American ones. They just laid the pipe and covered it, trying not to disturb the graves any more than necessary.

While the Ghost Trackers were present, a garden stake, about 6 feet long and bent at the end like a shepherd's staff that could be used as a plant hanger, levitated. It was in the corner with boxes in front of it. It rose up, catapulted up and over the boxes, and landed at their feet. Diane Lane and the crew of the show all saw it happen.

During another of their investigations, a coke can began walking down a perfectly flat bench. No one was near it. An English high school class was in with them on tour doing a workshop for a class paper but no one thought to take a picture.

During one tour a woman was mentally thinking, "Is there a spirit here?"

The following day, her husband saw some writing on her back. It appeared to be backwards and upside down so he had her stand with her back to a mirror and was able to read the writing. It said simply, "yes." The owner, Diane, said she thought she saw something but couldn't be sure. It had faded out somewhat by then. The writing came back as clear as before. The lady in question has since had the spirits follow her home as things are still happening to her. A good reason you should not try to interact with any entities you may encounter.

When the U.S. acquired North Florida in 1821, St. Augustine was the leading port of new territory and needed a harbor light to protect increased shipping. There was a small, three-story tower that may have been used for a beacon by the Spanish. They placed a temporary light atop this tower and planned to strengthen and outfit it with new lights and lens.

However, a government inspector sent to check out the tower felt it would be more practical to build a new one. The new tower rose seventy-three feet.

Incidentally, there have been women keepers. The first official woman keeper was Mrs. J. Andreau. She maintained the old lighthouse in the late 1850's, succeeding her husband who fell to his death while painting the tower. Perhaps his are the footsteps still heard on the stairs of the new lighthouse today. Many workers have also glimpsed a male figure ascending the stairs in the lighthouse.

One worker, who preferred not to be identified, told of going into the lighthouse one day when no one else was in it and noticing a rank smell. "It was like cigar smoke and bad body odor."

She then became aware of a muffled conversation. She could not make out any words but "it was a man and woman and they had a teasing tone in their voices, like maybe they were a little bit mad at one another."

The old lighthouse lighted the harbor until extinguished by the Confederate Army during the Civil War. Re-lit in 1867, it was increasingly threatened by erosion, prompting the construction of a new lighthouse on Anastasia Island. The old tower finally succumbed to the relentless tides in 1880.

Finding Florida's Phantoms

The new lighthouse was lit for the first time on October 15, 1874. The building was not completed without tragic costs. It took its toll in human life. Three young girls were drowned during construction, Mary and Eliza Pittee, the daughters of the construction supervisor, and an unknown African American girl. To this day, visitors and staff alike have glimpsed these girls near the building.

In spite of the harsh and difficult nature of the job, a keeper's pay was notoriously low. By the late 1800's, a keeper earned less than $600 per year and the assistant keeper, half that amount. The St. Augustine Keeper's position was a coveted one, perhaps partly since it was less isolated than many lighthouses and partly because the keeper's quarters were one of the best in the South.

The keeper's house completed 1876 was a two story brick duplex, with a basement, which was quite unusual in Florida. It was split down the middle, each side mirroring the other. Each had two rooms downstairs, the kitchen and eating area and the parlor. There were two bedrooms upstairs. In 1885, two summer kitchens were added in back of the house. Indoor plumbing came in 1907 and a small bathroom was squeezed between the bedrooms for both the keeper and the assistant. Water was supplied by means of roof gutters flowing into cisterns in the basement. The lighthouse didn't get electricity until 1936.

The keepers served faithfully with the only interruptions in service being during the Civil War and again during World War 11. President Roosevelt ordered the light dimmed because German Submarines would lie in wait for American vessels, which would be silhouetted by the lighthouse beacon and thus made an easy target for the German torpedoes. 1955 brought automation to the lighthouse and eliminated the need for a keeper.

The house was rented for a while, and then began to fall into disrepair. It was considered surplus government property. Finally came the most devastating blow, an early morning fire in the abandoned building. Dawn arose on a burned out hulk. Little remained of the once gracious home but the blackened walls and some of the foundation. It was hinted that the fire might have been arson but never proven. Could it have been started by one of the ghost children playing with matches?

The Junior League of St. Augustine began the Lighthouse Project 14 years ago. They purchased the house and grounds for $29,000 and signed a 99-year lease with the Coast Guard for the lighthouse. They have done a painstakingly accurate job of restoration. Then in 2003, the buildings were turned over to the city of St. Augustine to maintain.

Today, the Keeper's House is a museum housing lighthouse memorabilia. The parlor and kitchen/eating area of one side has been recreated. The other side is devoted to a souvenir shop. The upstairs that once housed the bedrooms is now a large ballroom, which can be rented for weddings or parties. One side of the basement houses museum displays. The other side contains a small viewing room with a video presentation about the history of the lighthouse. It is here that workers frequently sense a man's presence. Some have even seen him.

It is not just downstairs that strange things happen in the keeper's house either. The gift shop is located upstairs on the first floor. Many of the workers here have had unexplainable occurrences. Tina Guillotte closed one night. She set the alarm and went home. She also was the opening person the next day.

When she went in, she sensed something was wrong but she didn't realize what at first. Then as she stood at the register and counted money, it hit her. "All of the books in the store had been turned face down. I knew they had not been like that when I left. I was the last one out last night and first one in that morning."

Tina feels like it is one of the little girls since the incidents seem like a playful child's pranks. Another worker opened one morning to find all the disposable cameras and film piled in a stack like building blocks on the counter.

It is not just during the night that these things happen. Another worker, Pam Troll, was getting ready to close. Two other workers, Chris and Judy, were also present and saw the same things. She had counted the cash register and shut down the drawer. "I'm standing over by the counter. The cash register drawer popped open. Then a few minutes later, some little toys called Puddle Jumpers, one jumped off the counter. It was too far to have just fallen out. It went about seven feet, way too far to fall. We also have this little thing that when someone walks by it, the seagulls go around in a circle and plays music. We have some in back. Judy was on the other side of the stock room. For no reason it went off. Someone had walked past it but none of us were near it."

Pam also stated that all last summer workers would see someone go into the stock room and when they went in after them, no one would be there.

Directly in front of the keeper's house is Lighthouse Park. It contains a picnic and playground area, shaded by wind-bent oak trees, a boat dock, a fishing pier, tennis courts and delightful restaurant. At the Lighthouse restaurant you can dine inside in air conditioned comfort or enjoy the natural breezes on the veranda overlooking Salt Run. The outside definitely is more interesting with the view of water, boats and seabirds. You will soon be joined by one or more of the many cats who make the restaurant their home. They are very friendly and good mannered but most are not too proud to accept a handout if it's offered, although the owners ask you not to feed them for their own protection. Unlike some of their human counterparts, they do provide a useful service in return. You won't see any mice around this restaurant.

When you visit The Oldest City, a triumvirate of magnificent Victorian buildings stands out among the older Spanish styles: Flagler College, Lightner Museum and the Casa Monica Hotel. These all reflect the influence of the one man who, next to the early founders of the city, contributed more than anyone to creating the St Augustine of today.

The Hotel Ponce de Leon was Henry Flagler's first, and many say most magnificent, St Augustine hotel. It was designed and built by some of the nineteenth century's most notable designers, artists and architects in 1888. An imposing Spanish Renaissance building with its lavish interior, it was one of the grandest resorts of its time. Its guest list contained the cream of society, including three U.S. Presidents.

At the same time, he was building another hotel across the street, The Alcazar. Among its wonders, the Alcazar sported an indoor swimming pool, which you can still visit today. In 1947, Otto Lightner purchased the building and based his museum there. It is still Lightner Museum today.

Meantime, just down the block a Bostonian amateur architect, Franklin W. Smith, build The Casa Monica Hotel. It offered guests a Moorish Castle design, complete with turrets and an unbelievably lavish interior. Flagler purchased the hotel April 20, 1888 and it, too, became an immediate success.

In the 1960's it was converted the county courthouse but in 1999, it reverted to its former glory and is once again the Casa Monica Hotel. Many who have stayed state that they have heard voices, seen indents in the carpet as if someone is stepping on it and witnessed furniture shift positions inexplicably. Others have sighted a woman in green strolling around the hotel. The only thing strange about her is that she's not actually there. Visitors have glimpsed a man through the outside windows of the Henry Flagler Suite when the room was known to be empty. Some workers have seen a distinguished looking man in period clothing walking in the lobby, only to vanish when approached.

Flagler was a self-made millionaire, a partner of John D. Rockefeller. When his first wife Mary Harkness died, he married Ida Alice Shourds. Ida Alice was unstable to say the least. When she stabbed her doctor with her sewing scissors, Henry had her institutionalized in a cozy cottage where he settled five million dollars for her care. She swore that if he confined her to an institution, she would haunt him forever.

After neatly settling the problem of a homicidal maniac wife, Henry wanted to remarry. His choice for the third Mrs. Flagler was Mary Lily Kenan, an attractive lady thirty plus years his junior. However, the fly in the ointment was that both New York, where Henry maintained residency, and Florida, where he spent most of his time at this point, both forbade divorce from a mentally incapacitated person. Henry solved the problem by changing his residency to Florida, which was benefiting greatly from his entrepreneurial spirit. To further sweeten the pot, he made huge contributions to the winning political party. In 1901, the Florida legislature passed a law allowing divorce from mentally incapacitated persons. The law only remained on the books for ten day before it was repealed but Henry quickly divorced Ida Alice and married Mary Lily. Mary Lily won the marital sweepstakes. Henry died still married to her and left her the wealthiest woman in the country. In fact, she was the only woman in America wealthier than the Queen of England.

Flagler died in 1913 at the age of 93. His body was brought back on his railroad, Florida East Coast Railway, to lie in state at Ponce de Leon Hotel. That night a strange thing occurred. A caretaker cleaning around the coffin was suddenly frightened by a burst of wind in the otherwise calm day. It blew open the doors of the hotel and slammed shut the coffin cover. The terrified man cowered nearby as he observed a swirling glowing mist rise from the coffin towards the roof and then descend to the floor. When he regained enough courage to creep near the coffin again, he observed the image of Flagler's face in the tile. He is buried here in the Florida city that first captured his heart in a mausoleum at Memorial Presbyterian Church. However, he may not rest in peace. Many people have claimed to see his face reflected in the tiles in his first grand Florida hotel, the Ponce de Leon, now Flagler College. Some have seen him in the halls of Flagler College. Others have seen the spirit of Ida Alice waltzing around the ballroom with her imaginary Russian czar. Gentlemen, how many of you would like to be doomed to spend eternity with the one wife you wanted to get rid of?

Kathleen Walls

Henry Flagler wasn't the only one of the Robber Barons to live part of their life in St. Augustine. William G. Warden, a former partner of Flagler and Rockefeller, came here in 1887 with the original intent of investing in Flagler's railroad. However, when he realized the difficulties in the undertaking, he changed him mind. Instead, he decided that "He would not put a penny in the railroad but would build a large home here and watch Flagler go broke!"

The result was Historic Castle Warden. Today it's a Florida Historic Landmark, and home to St. Augustine's Ripley's Believe It or Not Museum. You might not be surprised to learn that the majestic gray stone "castle" has some things that go bump in the night and are even more unexplainable than Robert Ripley's oddities.

Lynda Stephens who works at the front desk told me of some of the stranger than fiction happenings. "One night we were counting the admissions drawer. It came out $144.49 short. That got us all upset. So the manager said, 'Lets count the gift shop then come back and maybe we can figure it out.' We counted the gift shop and it came out exactly $144.49 over. The two drawers never mingle. Never!"

Lynda also admitted to hearing many unusual noises in the old building. She is not comfortable being there late at night. There are reports that the spirit of a woman who died in a fire that swept the third and fourth floor still prowls the halls. The fire struck in 1944 and two women were trapped in the building. They wrapped themselves in wet towels to try to stave off the flames but still succumbed to the fumes. One of them, Betty Richerson, was found dead in a bathtub. One of the exhibits on that floor near the location where she was found has a mirror in the central area. People have claimed to see Betty's reflection in that mirror.

The Victorian era was a prosperous time for St. Augustine as you can see by all the Victorian houses and buildings, thanks mostly to Henry Flagler and his rich friends.

One of the many beautiful homes built during that period is the Casa Blanca Inn. The Mediterranean Revival home on the bay front was built by an Irish couple in 1914. The gentleman wanted to watch the sunrise from the porches. However, the couple both were quite fond of "the creature" and frequently had rowdy parties there. One day, the husband died.

The young widow was left with the large home but no money. She decided to turn it into a boarding house. She began throwing parties with rum flowing generously. She charged well for these parties and began to prosper.

Then a disastrous thing happened, the Volsted Act. Her parties would come to an end if she didn't do something. Being an enterprising lady, she befriended a group of rumrunners. One became her lover. Their ship would enter the bay front, dock and stay awhile with the merry widow.

All ointments are destined to have a few flies, however. These particular flies were the G-men sent to St. Augustine when the government learned it was a hotbed of rumrunners. This didn't faze the widow too much. Instead, she met the agents at the train and invited them to her boarding house. That way she could keep an eye on them. When they were in town, she would keep her windows walk dark. But when they were away on other business, she would wave a lantern from the highest part of the Widow's walk to let her lover know it was safe to come on in.

Finding Florida's Phantoms

After prohibition was repealed, her fickle lover no longer came to call. Rumor says that she still waved a lantern from the widow's walks until her dying day to no avail.

Even death seems not to have extinguished her lantern. Neighbors and sailors in the inlet claim to often see the ghostly lantern shedding its light across the waterfront. Some have even seen a dark shadowy figure in the widow's walk at night.

Obviously, the lady still feels that this is her "boarding house." One guest staying at the inn took some pictures. In one of them, she caught her own reflection in the mirror with her camera. Even though she was alone when she took the picture, standing right behind her in the photograph was a lady dressed in period clothing with a lantern in her hand.

There appears to be another resident still remaining in the inn from Victorian times. In those days, gentlemen would retire to the back porch to smoke their cigars. Today this "smoking porch" is an elegant bedroom. A female guest awoke one night to find a man sitting on the side of the bed smoking. When she awoke and saw him, he told her to "go back to sleep, everything is okay."

In fact so many of the city's old Bed and Breakfasts have ghost stories, it is the norm rather than the exception to share your room with a ghostly guest. Just next door to the Casa Blanca is the Casa de La Paz.

It was built in the same Mediterranean Revival style just one year later. Their resident spirit is a lady named Mabel. Mabel came to St. Augustine for her health with her husband in the early 1900's and they stayed at the inn. Her husband must have gotten tired of a sickly wife and left the inn one day and never came back. Well, as well bred Victorian ladies did not travel alone those days, Mabel just stayed on at the inn waiting for his return. He never came back and Mabel never left.

Guests report seeing her dressed in a long traveling dress with a broad brimmed hat and holding a small tapestry bag in her hand. She walks down the stairs, stops at the bottom of the landing and then returns upstairs.

Other guests tell of hearing a timid knock at their door and a voice whispering, "Is it time to go yet?"

When they open the door, no one is there

Another of Flagler's cohorts built himself a home in St. Augustine while he worked on the construction of the railroad and also on the Bridge of Lions. Walter Decker built what is now the Peace and Plenty Inn on Cedar St. around 1890.

In the ensuing century, the stately home fell into disrepair. Then in 1996, Court and Glena Terrell took on the task of restoring it to its former glory. They half jokingly say, "We have the scares to prove it!" Their remodeling was chronicled on the Home and Garden Television show *If Walls Could Talk*.

Their two sons, Clay and Casey, had an unearthly experience in the parlor. Clay says, "Casey was calling our dog, Dallas, and as he called, I heard a mocking female voice in the parlor repeating Casey's call, 'Dallas, Dallas.' This happened about 3 years ago when we were remodeling it. Dallas appeared confused and shaken by the echoing voice. She is usually a bold dog but was completely cowered and went running to Casey as if she was frightened."

Just next door at the Penny Farthing Inn, a similar style building also constructed by Mr. Decker, even stranger events are still taking place.

Ghost Victor turns on lights and televisions. He is a party type ghost and likes a good time. Guests have frequently thought there was a party going on in the parlor.

Once he turned the television on in a guest's room during the night. The husband and wife each thought the other one had.

Victor also "talks" to Connie. When she is undecided what she want to do he will mentally suggest, "Why don't you change the drapes?" or whatever ever he feels she should do.

The Penny Farthing Inn is also home to a ghostly yellow cat, Copper Penny, who belonged to a former owner. The cat died of old age under the house long ago but Connie frequently feels him rub against her legs and pat her with his paw. A guest once saw and heard him crying in his room. When he got up to let the cat out, it disappeared.

Of course, with all these prosperous law abiding citizens, there had to be a place to stow the others, the lawbreakers. From 1891 on into the 1950's, that place was the Old Jail. It is one of the few surviving 19th century jails and within its walls survives something else. Perhaps it is the vigilant spirit of old Sheriff Perry, St. Johns County's 7-foot tall first sheriff. Maybe it is Slim Jackson, one of the early deputies. Or it could even be a man hanged on the gallows still displayed out behind the Old Jail. Whoever it is has been heard by more than one visitor to the site. They hear voices, sometimes male and sometimes female. In addition to prisoners of both sexes kept in different sections of the jail, the sheriff and his wife and family lived on the premises. Mrs. Perry cooked and served the inmates in the jail dining room.

Jeff Reynolds from Ghost Tracker Radio and his crew went to the Old Jail. They heard people banging on the bars and cell doors slamming. They stated that there seemed to be a crowd of entities there.

The St. Johns-St. Augustine Chamber of Commerce has always boasted about the Nation's Oldest City. Now it's bragging about the newest addition to the county's attractions, World Golf Village. For golfers and non-golfers alike, it provides a world of fun.

Everyone can enjoy the Golf Hall of Fame. It is best described as a celebration of the game. Laid out like a golf course in 18 exhibits, many of them interactive, it traces the history of golf.

The Tower Shrine invites you to ascend to its 190-foot peak. Arising like a beacon, the tower is a monument to golf legends, living and dead. The multi-windowed shrine has a shimmering prism at its peak creating brilliant shafts of light that reflect off the crystal plates honoring each member of the Hall of Fame. The tower also gives a great view of the village. In front, the Walk of Champions circles the lake and fountain in the middle of the village.

Next door, the IMAX theater allows you to view films like *Alaska: Spirit of the Wild* and *Dolphins* on a six story high screen. The impact is the next best thing to being in the midst of a raging blizzard deep in Alaska's wilderness or deep beneath the ocean playing with a wild dolphin.

Finding Florida's Phantoms

Every Friday during the summer, the Village treats its guests to a free concert and fireworks around the lake. Just bring your lawn chairs and dancing shoes and enjoy.

You will also find art shows, antique auto cruise-ins, and lots of other family fun in the village. Lots of delightful little shops too.

If you venture south down Highway 13 along the river, there are two unique restaurants. Scuttlebutt is located on Trout Creek. A bit farther along you will find Six-Mile Marina and their Outback Crab Shack. Here you can enjoy seafood in a rustic setting on the waterfront.

One treat that cost nothing is a drive along the St. Johns River at sunset. The view is fabulous. You may spot an alligator or a blue heron. You can insure sighting these at the Alligator Farm on Anastasia Island.

Among the priceless memories you will carry home from your visit is the sight of the sun dipping into the waters of the river. It paints sky and water every imaginable shade of red. When viewed through draped Spanish moss, it will be a perfect finish to an unforgettable vacation experience whether or not you catch a glimpse of one of the oldest city's ethereal residents. However, if you are intent of spotting one of these elusive phantoms, you couldn't find a better hunting ground. St. Augustine has more ghosts per square foot in its ancient historic section than any other place in the country.

Contacts:

Peace and Plenty Inn
87 Cedar Street
St. Augustine, Florida 32084
United States
904 829 8209
1-877-468-3651
FAX: 904-829-8209
peaceandplentyinn1890@hotmail.com
http://www.peaceandplentyinn.com

St. Francis Inn Bed & Breakfast
279 St. George Street, St. Augustine, Florida 32084
Toll-free: 1-800-824-6062
Tel: (904) 824-6068 • Fax: (904) 810-5525
Email: info@stfrancisinn.com
www.stfrancisinn.com

Penny Farthing Inn
83 Cedar St
St. Augustine, FL 32084
(800) 395-1890
www.pennyfarthinginn.net

O. C. White's Seafood & Spirits
(904) 824-0808
118 Avenida Menendez
St. Augustine, FL

Scarlett O'Hara's
70 Hypolita Street, St. Augustine, FL 32084
(904) 824-6535

Mission of Nombre de Dios
27 Ocean Avenue
Saint Augustine, FL 32084
 (904) 824.2809
www.shrineshop.com

Original Ghost Tours of St. Augustine
(888) 461-1009
Info@ghosttoursofstaugustine.com
http://www.ghosttoursofstaugustine.com/

Castillo de San Marcos
One South Castillo Drive
St. Augustine, FL 32084
904-829-6506
904-823-9388 fax

Fort Matanzas National Monument
8635 HWY A1A South
St. Augustine, FL 32086
904-471-0116
904-471-7605 fax

Old Florida Museum
254 A San Marco Avenue
St. Augustine, FL 32084
(904)824-8874
(800)813-3208 toll-free
904-824-6848 fax
www.oldfloridamuseum.com

Ripley's Believe It or Not
19 San Marco Ave.
St. Augustine, FL 32084
(904) 824-1606
(904) 829-1790 fax
www.ripleys.com/bion/staug.html

Finding Florida's Phantoms

St. Augustine Alligator Farm
999 Anastasia Blvd.
St. Augustine, FL 32080
904-824-3337
877-966-7275 toll-free
904-829-6677 fax
www.alligatorfarm.com

St. Augustine Lighthouse and Museum
81 Lighthouse Avenue
St. Augustine, FL 32080
(904) 829-0745
(904) 808-1248 fax
www.staugustinelighthouse.com

World Golf Hall of Fame
One World Golf Place
St. Augustine, FL 32092
904-940-4123
(800) WGV-GOLF
(904) 940-4390 fax
www.wghof.org

World Golf Village IMAX Theater
1 World Golf Place
St. Augustine, FL 32092
(904) 940-IMAX
(904) 940-4390 fax

Harry's seafood Bar and Grill
46 Avenida Menendez
St. Augustine, FL 32084
(904) 387-0304
hookedonharrys.com

Lake City and Gainesville

Driving into Florida from Georgia on I-95, Lake City is the gateway to the state. This gateway city began as a Seminole village called Alpata Telophka, Alligator Town. No, it wasn't named for the reptile that people expect to see once they cross the state line. It was named in honor of a young Seminole warder, Alligator.

By 1830, an American settlement had established itself next to the Seminole village and used the same name for their village. It wasn't until December 1858 that the name of Lake City was chosen. Mrs. Elex Young picked it because of the many lakes in the area. The town was incorporated the next year.

The area is best remembered in history for The Battle of Olustee, which took place at Ocean Pond near Lake City on February 20, 1864. It was the largest military engagement to occur in Florida. The Union forces were trying to cut their opponents supply lines and reach Tallahassee. The battle resulted in a Confederate victory when they stopped the Federal troops but they failed pursuing the retreating Union army and so did not capitalize on the victory. Each year in February, a re-enactment is held at Olustee, the scene of the battle

The Olustee site had recently drawn "ghost hunters" after photographs taken at the re-enactment several years ago showed orbs over the battlefield. Several visitors also physically saw the strange glowing lights there. They seem to reoccur annually at the re-enactments. Could it be the spirits of the war dead still wandering the old battlefield?

Lake City grew rapidly and by the early 1900's it had become an important railroad junction serving the Seaboard Air Line, Atlantic Coast Line, Georgia Southern, and the Florida Railroad.

A good place to start a tour of Lake City is the Columbia County Historical Museum on Hernando Street. It tells the history of the area from before the first settlers to present day.

Another good reason to visit the museum is its resident ghost. Cora Vinzant, the family's 18-year-old daughter, is said to have died of yellow fever in an upstairs bedroom in 1892, just a day before she would have graduated from Lake City

Finding Florida's Phantoms

Institute. There is good reason to believe she still inhabits the museum that was once her home.

When you visit, talk to Museum director John Shoemaker, he may be unsure about the existence of "Cora" in the museum but he will tell you things get inexplicably moved around inside the museum.

At least one museum volunteer has no doubts that there is a presence in the building. She was working alone in it and heard someone distinctly call her name from upstairs.

Shoemaker admits strange things do happen in the museum. Once at Christmas time, there were lots of little Nutcracker figures on display. One morning when he came in, all of the figures were turned to face the wall. "Some of them were pretty ugly," he admitted.

Chairs are another moving object there. They move from place to place with no apparent cause. One rocker is seen to rock when no one is in it. No one earthly that is!

Shoemaker also had contact with several other ghosts. They reside in the Old Blanche Hotel on Marion Avenue. No longer in use, it was once a fine hotel. Now it is on the national Register of Historic Places. He was the first person to go on the second floor after the hotel had been boarded up for years.

New owners bought it and wanted him to catalogue and value some of the items stored there. He heard voices, doors opening and closing and footsteps. They also seemed to be coming from the empty third floor. He finally concluded they were not going to harm him so he just left them alone.

With the decline of the railroads, Lake City has lost its reputation as a "hustle and bustle" city. What it had become is vastly more attractive.

It hosts the Florida Sports Hall of Fame, believed by many to be the best state facility in the nation. It honors every aspect of sports available in Florida.

As in all modern cities, it has a well-equipped fire department. This one has something a lot of other fire departments don't have, its own ghost.

A group of psychic investigators, called in because of items moving around on their own, got clear pictures of orbs. In fact, many people using different digital cameras got pictures of the orbs. When they were downloaded into a computer, distinct faces could be seen.

The building had once been used for funerals so perhaps that is where the spirits are coming from.

Looking for a place to stay that has ghosts? Between Lake City and Gainesville at High Springs, you will find Grady House. It was built in 1917 as the town's first bakery. It later became a boarding house during the peak of the railroad boom. It has been restored to its original charm and is now on the National Historic Register.

Kirk Eppenstein and Tony Boothby bought the place several years ago and turned it into a Bed and Breakfast.

At first, they didn't believe any of the ghostly rumors but as things began to occur that could not be explained any other way, they were forced to accept that they had not one but two ghosts.

One of the first things that convinced them were the chess pieces being moved to a particular square and another piece placed on top of it. No matter how many times they were put away, they always returned to that spot. Another occurrence that helped convince them was the sound of heavy footsteps on the floor above them when no one was in the room.

The knowledge of the female ghost came when several visitors would tell of being tucked into bed by a motherly middle-aged lady. Some have actually seen her. Often there is a strong perfume smell.

The Red Room is the room where the woman is most often seen. She is seen as a woman in a nightgown, often brushing her hair. In spite of, or perhaps because of this, the Red Room is the most popular room at the Inn,

No one died in the house as far as the owners can determine but Mrs. Grady did die in a tragic car accident.

If you prefer to stay at a haunted place in Gainesville, consider the Sweetwater Branch Inn. The inn is composed of two magnificent old mansions, Cushman-Colson house and McKenzie House.

The McKenzie House was built in 1895. Mary Pound McKenzie moved there with her first husband who died in 1917. She married Reid McKenzie in 1925. Mr. McKenzie was only thirty-four so it is no surprise that his spirit still roams the house. Cornelia Holbrook bought it and turned it into the Sweetwater Branch Inn in 1995.

Guests in the attic rooms have awaken with a heavy feeling on their chest. Could it just be coincidence that Mr. McKenzie died of bronchial pneumonia in his sleep?

Another Bed and Breakfast not far from there also houses a famous haunt. Just south of Gainesville, there is a pillared three-story brick mansion on Cholokka Boulevard in the heart of Micanopy, the Mecca for antique hunters.

The Herlong Mansion Bed & Breakfast has attracted the attention of many ghost hunters. The tragic story of Inez has been told numerous times.

The Herlong's acquired the simple farmhouse built in 1845. They transformed it into a magnificent Southern mansion. Mr. Herlong's children, all of whom were supposed to inherit the home, fought bitterly over it when he died.

Inez Herlong Miller won the court battle but lost her siblings' love in the process. They refused to set foot in the house again. Inez died there of a heart attack.

Since then, many people have seen and heard Inez. The sightings are particularly frequent in "May's Room," the room of a sister she had fought bitterly to gain possession of the home.

Gainesville, like Lake City, began in the mid 1800's. It was founded on September 6, 1853 on sixty acres of land purchased from Major James B. Bailey, a cotton plantation owner and former County Treasurer. His own house is the oldest in Gainesville, begun in 1848 and completed in 1854. It was restored in the early 1980's and is now a rest home.

During the Civil War, Gainesville was the site of an important Confederate storehouse. In the early 1900's, it was an important railroad town and the fourth largest city in Florida.

Shortly after the war, it began to take on its present day character as a college town. Education began to come to the forefront. Gainesville Academy, the town's first school was joined with Ocala's East Florida Seminary in 1866. Union Academy, the area's first Black school, opened in 1867. These paved the way for the University of Florida being founded there in 1906.

Finding Florida's Phantoms

College towns seem to attract the spirits. Dorms and university buildings often have fascinating stories of long dead previous inhabitants that still prowl the halls of learning. University of Florida is no exception.

Beatty Towers is rumored to be inhabited by the spirit of a female student who committed suicide here by jumping off the tower. Her reason is believed to be an unwanted pregnancy. Many of the women who live in the dorm have seen her apparition gliding through the halls at night. Still others have heard unexplained noises there.

Some people have said the suicide did not occur in Beatty towers at all but at an apartment complex a few miles away. They still acknowledge activity in the building but attribute it to a boy who died here of alcohol poisoning.

Thomas Hall Dormitory is another spot on the campus with unexplainable occurrences. It is one of the oldest buildings on campus, dating back to the early days of the school. It was once used for classrooms and the resident spirit is believed to be a former employer, perhaps a janitor since the noises heard are loud bangings from the radiators when they are not in use and should not be making any sounds.

Norman Hall, which is now the College of Education but used to be used to be the P.K. Young School, is haunted by the presence of several young children who were killed in an elevator accident. The sounds of childish laughter and voices are often heard on the third floor. The old elevator is still there. Perhaps that is why the children are tied to the place.

One unusual research institution is located in Gainesville. The American Institute of Parapsychology, headed by Dr. Andrew Nichols, is there. The Institute investigates many strange phenomena. One of the places Dr. Nichols has had good reason to investigate is the Hippodrome State Theater. It is reportedly haunted by a Lady in Blue.

The theater's General Manager, Mark Sexton, claims he has never seen anything unusual himself but states, "Other actors and employees have. There was one woman, an employee and an actress in many of the productions, who witnessed a woman dressed in a blue gown from the late nineteen hundred's while she was working late at night in the theater. The figure was gliding about a foot above the floor."

Many others have heard footsteps and voices, experienced cold spots and even seen apparitions. Dr. Nichols investigated it in 1996 and confirmed that there was more than one presence in the old theater. Strangely enough, the places where his team found the strongest energy corresponded to the places the woman has been sighted.

Perhaps they stem from the time when the stately columned building was the Alachaua courthouse and a gallows stood in back. Justice was swift in those days. There is a story of a woman who came to seek her husband but he had already been hanged when she arrived. Is she still searching in vain for him?

Another spot that is well known in Gainesville was a local institution known as the Purple Porpoise for decades. Last year, it closed down and was replaced by a new club, Gator City. Since it is in the same building, only time will tell if the name change and sale got rid of the ghosts.

The problem began back in 1965 when a young woman, Kathryn Elizabeth Olivera, was brutally murdered in the upstairs bathroom. The place was called

College Inn then. The area where the crime occurred has long been a storeroom in the Purple Porpoise but employees have complained of strange activities there,

One janitor, who had just cleaned a hallway, turned to find a 2x4 sitting in the middle of the hall. Obviously, he had not cleaned around it. It just materialized there for no reason.

Televisions in the bar and restaurant come on all by themselves. People who enter the room often feel the two presences. Hers, frightened and confused. His, pure evil.

Whether the phenomena will continue in the new incarnation only time will tell.

Contacts:

Lake City, Florida Tourist and Convention Information
435 N.W. Hall of Fame Dr.
Lake City, FL 32055
386-758-1312
877-746-4778
Lake City, Florida Visitors Bureau Website:
www.springs-r-us.org

Gainesville Convention and Visitors bureau
http://www.visitgainesville.net/
(866) 778.5002
(352) 374.5260
jop@visitgainesville.net

Florida Sports Hall of Fame
106 Hall of Fame Drive, off Highway 90 West.
386-758-1310

Columbia County Historical Museum
105 South Hernando Street
386-755-9096

Herlong Mansion
Linda Barrett & Mark Gregg, Innkeepers
402 N.E. Cholokka Boulevard
P.O. Box 667
Micanopy, Florida 32667
(352) 466-3322
info@herlong.com

Finding Florida's Phantoms

Hippodrome State Theatre
25 SE 2nd Place
Gainesville FL 32601
box office: (352) 375-4477
administration: (352) 373-5968
hipp@thehipp.org

Gator City (Formerly Purple Porpoise)
1728 W. University Ave
Gainesville FL, USA

Sweetwater Branch Inn
625 East University Avenue
Gainesville, Florida 32601
(352)373-6760
(800) 595-7760
Fax:
(352) 371-3771
reserve@sweetwaterinn.com

Amelia Island Lighthouse
Photo by KathleenWalls

Finding Florida's Phantoms

Top: Palace Saloon in Fernandina Beach
Bottom: Kingsley Plantatiion north of Jacksonville
Photos by Kathleen Walls

Top: Casa Marina on Jacksonville Beach
Bottom: Fort Matanzas, St. Augustine's "back door"
Photos by Kathleen Walls

Penny Farthing Inn in St. Augustine.
Photo by Kathleen Walls

Olustee's monument to the fallen soldiers who fought there.
Photo by Kathleen Walls

Finding Florida's Phantoms

Central Ocala

Ponce de Leon first claimed this central Florida pineland for Spain. The beauty of the rolling pine forest and scrubland make it attractive for both human and wildlife habitation.

Ocala was the state's fifth largest city in the 1900's. Since then it has lost its metropolis standing but still offers many of the amenities larger cities do. It is the center of Florida's "Horse Country" just about an hour drive north of Disney's Magic Kingdom.

Just outside the city of Ocala lies another "Magic Kingdom." Mother Nature rules this kingdom. It's the Ocala National Forest, 430,000 scenic acres of the most diverse terrain imaginable. It contains highlands, swamps, 600 lakes, countless ponds, 23 streams and springs of clear crystal water. It's bounded by the slow, dark waters of the Oklawaha River on the west and the larger, faster moving St. Johns River on the east. It is the oldest national forest east of the Mississippi.

The flora and fauna of the area is diverse. You will explore oak hammocks and vast stands of sand pine. You will encounter large live oaks, scrub oak, longleaf pine, sand pine, loblolly pine, pigmy hickory, dogwood, magnolia, sable palm, palmetto, and countless other trees.

The other plant life is equally interesting. The Resurrection Fern grows in the crevices of trees. In dry seasons it looks brown and dead, but after a good rain, it springs to life again, green and vibrant.

Deer Moss is a type of lichen found in many areas of the forest. It resembles gray-green sponge, growing close to the ground. Even the bright pinkish red markings on the trunks of trees are a type of lichen called Foliose.

The forest is home to a multitude of animals. The shy black bears reside there. They are rarely seen as they avoid people. The bobcat is another resident you probably won't see too often. The white tail deer can be observed frequently. The white squirrel can only be found in Juniper Springs' area. The gray squirrel is seen all over the forest, as are armadillos, raccoons, hares, gopher tortoises and many other species.

Eagles and ospreys are not an uncommon sight. Many types of egret and heron and dozens of other wading birds live in the forest. The Florida scrub jay lives in the young stands of sand pine. As the stands grow older and form a canopy, the jay moves to a new area of young pines. Many other birds migrate through the area seasonally.

The reptile population is well represented, from the numerous alligators to the rare eastern indigo snake. The Indigo Snake, which is an endangered species, is quite an actor. If threatened, he will flatten his head, hiss, vibrate his tail and even strike. It's all a bluff; his bite is harmless.

Another place that may or may not be harmless is the cottage in Oklawaha on Lake Weir, where Ma Barker and her son Fred were killed in a FBI shootout that lasted for hours. Many people have seen Ma Barker still sitting on the porch as she did in life.

Each January, the Lake Weir holds a re-enactment. In case any of you are not familiar with the story, it happened like this.

The Barker/Karpis gang had found things a bit too hot in the mid-west after several kidnapping operations. Doc, one of the sons, was captured. Kate Barker and her oldest son, Fred, move to the Oklawaha hideout.

The government agents located them and on January 16, 1935, after one of the bloodiest shootouts in federal history, Fred was killed with his machine gun in hand. Ma was also found dead with three bullets in her. Since J. Edgar Hoover did not want the FBI to have a reputation for shooting old ladies, a story was circulated that Kate Barker shot herself after seeing her favorite son gunned down.

Also, in order to deflect blame, Hoover claims that Ma Barker was in fact the head of the gang. This was not supported by any factual evidence. In fact, she had no criminal record at all. The only "crime" she was ever guilty of was protecting her sons. The "Ma Barker" legend was created after federal agents shot her to death.

Kate and Fred Barker were laid out for public display in a local funeral parlor after the shooting. Perhaps she is still lurking around the old homestead to protest the injustice she feels was committed to her.

This is not the only haunted place in the forest. The "Rainbow People," a group of modern-day traveling gypsies or perhaps remnants of the hippies, have told of seeing phantom children that giggle and play in the forest glens.

One common legend in the forest is that of a man wandering up and down the country roads. He is wearing a long hooded black coat pulled up to cover his face. Travelers frequently have called local ranger stations and police to reporting this man lying on the side of the road. Sometimes he is seen walking, and sitting on the guardrails of bridges late at night.

I was camping one July at Farles Prairie. It's a primitive campground with the same facilities as Buck Lake but it will accommodate larger RV's.

Farles Prairie has some interesting stories, which get passed down from the old regular campers to new ones, as they visit around the campfires in the evening.

Don and Melvina Goulab have been camping there regularly for over 35 years. At that time, only the beach side was for public camping. The forest side was occupied by an enlisted men's club for the Navy. They recall often awakening in the night, to find a sailor and his girl sitting around their campfire.

As we sat around a campfire toasting marshmallows with the Goulabs - their grandson Arthur, James and Vivian Merrill and their Chinese Pug Mollie - Don recalled the night a drunk got abandoned at the campground. Apparently,

Finding Florida's Phantoms

the man's wife or girl friend left him there and took off with another man. The rejected lover bemoaned his fate by beating on other people's campers and crying loudly "My ole yadie's gone! My ole yadie's gone!"

He wanted someone to help him track her down. Instead, several of the campers bundled him in a car and took him to the sheriff in Aster. The unhappy lawman wanted them to take the lovesick drunk back to the campground since it was in a different jurisdiction. No one would do that so the sheriff had to deal with the situation.

No campfire get together would be complete without a wild animal story. Melvina told about the time she was walking on the road late in the evening and saw "two bears holding hands."

Lots of people have seen bears on the road but no one else saw them holding hands. Maybe the bears were not real but phantom bears since this area has all kinds of other ghosts anyway.

If camping is not your thing and you want to stay where there is hot and cold running water along with any other amenity you might desire, including hot and cold running ghosts, you have several choices in Ocala.

Seven Sisters Inn in Ocala's historic district is a place where you can be sure of plenty of nurturing. Bonnie Moreland and her husband, Ken Oden, and the rest of the staff at the two gracious Victorian manors that comprise the inn are always looking out for your comfort. But they have some help from a couple of benevolent spirits.

One entity, the woman they call Judy, resides in the original Seven Sisters, a graceful Queen Anne style home built in 1888. An earlier home at that location had previously been destroyed by fire. The presence made itself felt soon after Ken and Bonnie purchased the house. It had been struck by lightning shortly before they acquired it and had extensive water damage. Both of them sensed "something." The previous owners were unhelpful. In fact, they hung up on Bonnie when she called. Strange thing happened in the house. Bonnie found that one table she put on the third floor would be thrown around. "You could hear all kind of commotion downstairs. It was actually flipped upside down. After the third time, I moved it downstairs. Then it was fine."

The first incident that really caught her attention happened at one of the first events held at the inn. "We had a small wedding just about a month after we owned it. Just about ten people down in the lobby. We tried to light candles on long candlesticks. Each time they would be blown out. Finally, the candlesticks started to fall and were thrown across the floor."

They thought the mystery was solved when their handyman actually spotted a presence. He was repairing some rotting wood on the balcony. As he worked, another worker came on the balcony and handed him a hammer that he needed. The handyman came down and asked, "Who's the other workman you have here?" Mystified, Bonnie replied, "There's no other workman." The man then described the "other workman" as having a mustache and wearing old-fashioned clothes and a tool belt. But there were still more invisible inhabitants.

Bonnie once had a glimpse of a female presence. She recalls the incident. "I was going from the kitchen to Bonnie's Room on the first floor. This is the only time in thirteen years I actually saw her. She appeared to be from the civil war era. She was wearing a long gray skirt and a white blouse. Her hair was up in a bun."

There are also supposed to be two children but Bonnie had never noticed their presence.

For a while after acquiring the second house, an equally charming "Painted Lady" next door to the original inn, Bonnie thought there were no spirits in it. However early in 2002, she was working in the India Room and distinctly heard a man yell, "Hey." She knew all the guest were out for the evening, "So I went out into the hall thinking it was someone who had come in downstairs and was looking to see if anyone was around. No one was there. About ten minutes later, I heard a woman moan. I don't know if they were talking or what but it was very definite."

Bonnie later visited a psychic in Cassadaga. The woman told her some very accurate personal things. So when she began talking about the inn and its presences, she paid a lot of attention. "She told me that there was a man, an Indian doctor, from India not an American Indian, who lived in this house. A Ph.D., not a medical doctor. And he lived in this room in the 1800's.

"She also told me that the spirit in the first house was connected to the land not the house. 'There was a battlefield here then and a hospital. The woman came here to nurse her husband and she stayed on to help others.'"

Even without the attraction of the ghosts, the Seven Sisters is a delightful wonderland of exotic places and long ago times. The rooms in the original house are decorated in honor of the original owners of the house. There are extravagant touches of Victorian splendor mixed with the most exquisitely designed baths. The loft suite where the presence is most often felt is done in a seaside motif.

The second house is the Seven Sisters Around the World. Along with the India Room, there are many other treasure trove rooms. One of the most interesting pieces is a two hundred-year-old door from Bali. However, both the houses are stuffed with unique finds from all over the world. Country Inns Bed & Breakfast Magazine named Seven Sisters Inn the "Inn of the Month." The Inn also won an award for "Best Restoration Project." It is listed on the National Register of Historic Places.

The Ritz Historical Inn is another historic Ocala landmark. Built in 1925, it's a Mediterranean Style landmark in the city. It was one of the city's first apartment building during the Florida Land Boom. It is listed in the National Registry of Historic Places.

Today, it is one of Ocala's favorite inns. No wonder. It offers all the amenities found in the best hotels as well as keeping a masseuse on staff with two private massage rooms. Its Pavilion is able to accommodate weddings or other functions and the entire package is surrounded by a lush courtyard with a sparkling fountain. The mosaic tile swilling pool is a treat on Florida's hot days.

It has carefully preserved its old style elegance while adding modern amenities. One thing it has been careful to provide is ample protection against the possibility of a fire in the hotel. It was due to an unfortunate fire that it has acquired its permanent guest.

Back in the boom days, it was a hangout for rich fashionable New Yorkers escaping the big city for some fun in the sun. One socialite threw a party filled

Finding Florida's Phantoms

with laughing northerners that ended in tragedy. A fire broke out and a woman and her two dogs were killed in the fire. The room the party was in, Room No. 211, is called the Rose Room. Many people have said that the lights go off and on by themselves and the door always seems to stick even though it is well maintained and has no reason not to swing freely.

To this day, it is rumored you can hear the sound of a party and people rushing to escape the flames.

Ocala is horse country. Thoroughbred horse farms stud the countryside. The county is home to some of the most beautiful horses you have ever laid eyes upon but there is one horse you better hope you never see.

In 1891, Beatrice Marean wrote a book called *The Tragedies of Oak Hurst*. It told an old Marion county story about the eternal triangle.

It was based on what happened around the time of the Civil War at Oak Hurst, once a beautiful old plantation in Ocala. The owner married the woman he loved. Her name was Mercedes. Unfortunately, his cousin also loved the same woman. When the jealous cousin realizes she will never be his, he kills her while she is out riding. The distraught husband finds his beloved dead and brings her into the mansion, lays her on the bed and shoots himself there besides her. Later that night Mercedes' riderless white horse comes home.

The old mansion on Citrus Street has long crumbled to make way for more modern developments but the legend of the white horse is still around. If you see a handsome riderless phantom horse near Ocala in the moonlight, beware. Seeing the horse presages death or another great tragedy will befall you.

Just east of Ocala is Silver Springs. The city and the famed amusement park are both known by that name. It was a revered place to the early Native Americans who called the area with the springs Ocali.

It didn't take long for the American settlers to discover the beauty of the place. It was soon wrest from the natives. However, all of the glass-bottomed boats that cruise the river today are named in honor of the Indian chiefs who first revered this beautiful land and its crystal rivers and springs. Hubbart Hart is credited with bringing the first "tourists" into the area via his Hart Lines, a stagecoach line that connected the area with Palatka and Tampa, in 1860.

With the invention of the glass bottom boat in 1878 by Hullum Jones, the underwater beauty was opened up for all to glimpse, not just the divers. One of the most beautiful underwater grottos is The Bridal Chamber. Local legend states that if you look carefully, you may see two figures in an eternal embrace beneath the clear waters of the Silver River.

The legend has come down from the days the Native Americans roamed the area. The story goes that once two local tribes warred on one another. Winonah and Oklawaha were members of the warring tribes who were in love. Chief Okehumpkee, Winonah's father, forbade the union and the two lovers threw themselves into the spring and drowned.

Because of its pristine beauty, Silver Springs became *the place* to shoot jungle movies. In the 1930's and 40's, six of the Tarzan movies with Johnny Weissmuller were shot there. Many others were also shot there including the 1954 horror classic, *The Creature from the Black Lagoon*.

Kathleen Walls

Strangely enough, the story reflects an old forest legend. The same creature shows up all over south and central Florida but here, especially when you walk alone, in the deep woods of Ocala National forest, it seems possible, even probable.

Some call it the skunk ape, skunk man or moss man. Whatever it is, people have spotted it roaming around the Ocala National Forest. It is some sort of bigfoot-like creature.

According to Earl DeBary, curator of artifacts for the Marion County Museum of History, "It's supposed to be a creature covered with fur, about seven-feet tall, that walks upright and weighs about 450 pounds."

Some people believe it is a missing link between man and ape; others believe it is some kind of monster as the Creature from the Black Lagoon was supposed to be. Sightings have been predominately around the Juniper Springs area. Whatever it is, it has been hanging around these woods for a long time. DeBary, who is over 60, recalls hearing the tale as a youngster.

Ocala and its surrounding area, like its phantoms, are unique and definitely worth a visit no matter whether your taste run to outdoors woodsy stuff, horses, or urban pleasures.

Contacts:

Ocala National Forest
www.southernregion.fs.fed.us/florida/recreation/index_oca.shtml

Ritz Historical Inn
(888) 382-9390
1205 East Silver Springs Boulevard
Ocala, Florida 34470
http://www.ritzhistoricinn.com

Seven Sisters Inn Bed and Breakfast
820 SE Fort King Street ~ Ocala, Florida (FL) 34471
Telephone: 352-867-1170 ~ Fax: 352-876-5266 ~ Toll Free: 800-250-3496
sevensistersinn@msn.com
www.sevensistersinn.com

Silver Springs
5656 E. Silver Springs Blvd.
Silver Springs, FL 34488
353-236-2121
Info@silversprings.com
http://www.silversprings.com/index-flash.htm

Finding Florida's Phantoms

Appleton Museum of Art
4333 NE Silver Springs Blvd.
Ocala, FL 34470-5000
(352) 236-7100
Fax (352) 236-7136
jorme@appleton.fsu.edu
http://www.appletonmuseum.org/

Marion County Museum of History
307 SE 26th Terrace
Silver Springs, FL 34488
 (352) 629-2773

Ocala Chamber of Commerce
110 East Silver Springs Boulevard, on Ocala's Downtown Historic Square.
Ocala, FL US 34470
(352) 629-8051
Fax (352) 629-7651
ourguest@ocalacc.com

Eleven

Daytona Beach

Daytona Beach is best known as a haven for powerful machines, both two wand four wheeled, and the sun worshiping college students who converge on the "World's Most Beautiful Beach" each spring. The days are sun drenched and active and the nights are lively and earthy. This is the last place you would expect to encounter the dead and the unearthly. But the spirits are there just below the surface, a constant reminder to the racers, the bikers, and the tanners, that life is short and eternity long. So enjoy the fun in the sun but don't forget what lurks in the night.

One of Daytona Beach's best-documented ghosts "lives" at the Halifax Historical Museum. Marian has been manifesting herself in the old bank turned museum since shortly after her death in 1979, when her family donated her wedding dress and many of her personal items to the museum. Tall, slender and dark haired, Marian had loved her clothes. She had been married in that dress in 1898 and perhaps it was her favorite item of clothing. Her wedding day may well have been the happiest day of her life. For whatever the reason, she has chosen to remain with her things at the museum. The first person to report a sighting was a policeman walking his beat in the 1980's. He reported seeing the foggy image of a woman wearing a long white dress among the displays in the back of the museum. Since then others have seen, heard and sensed her presence.

Cheryl Atwell, the museum's director, has had her share of ghostly encounters. When she first came to work at the museum, the then director warned her of the ghost. She told Cheryl that the presence was quite mischievous. But it was a while before she felt the presence herself. Since then, she has observed things that are put in a certain place disappear and turn up some place different. Lights would go on or off mysteriously. Although she had never actually seen the spirit, she has observed her actions on more than one occasion. Once during a candlelit tour of the building, something kept pushing the glass covers off the candles and blowing out the flames. About forty guests, including a reporter from a local newspaper at the tour, all observed the glass chimneys flying off and

Finding Florida's Phantoms

crashing to the floor when no one was around them. We concluded the ghost was afraid of fire. It was the same night that Cheryl's husband, Tim, went back to the break room, housed in an old vault in the rear of the building. Cheryl explained, "He didn't want to turn the light on because the candlelight tour group was nearby. He reached into the refrigerator to get a soft drink and when he turned around, there she was. He felt a chill and saw a misty column of white. He rushed back to the front, his eyes wide as saucers. 'Honey, I just saw your ghost.'"

It was at another function that someone else saw her. One of the volunteer's daughters, Margo, went back to the lady's room. When she entered, she glanced at the mirrors and saw a woman dressed in turn of the century clothing staring back at her. She turned and looked around. No one else was in the rest room. She rushed back up front and told the others what she had seen. A group then returned to the restroom to see if the presence was still there. It was not.

There had always been a possibility the entity was one of several people. One candidate was a former president of the historic society who was robbed and killed while working late. Two other possibilities were bank workers who had died on the premises. One was a young teller in her twenties who died while working in her cage. The other woman was older. She had felt sick, went upstairs to lie down, and then had a fatal heart attack.

Cheryl credits Margo's sighting to identify the ghost as Marian. "Margo was able to describe the clothes in detail and the period is right for Marian."

She noted that the presence is becoming more active lately. "Perhaps she likes all the improvements we are making in the building or maybe it's that more people are coming in to visit the museum." She added, "For whatever reason, the ghost seems to like the back of the building near the vault or the lady's room."

Joan Meyers, Cheryl's personal assistant, usually arrives first in the morning. She has frequently heard the swish of Marian's taffeta skirt and seen a blur out of the corner of her eye. One morning just after arriving, she heard footsteps. Thinking Cheryl had arrived early, she called out "Hi, Cheryl." But when she looked up, she was astonished. "No one was there but both doors to the credenza by my desk just flew open."

The beach side's oldest house is also equipped with its resident spirit. The house is known as "Lillian's Place." Pat Bennett, the granddaughter of the original owner, at one time rented out a separate apartment in the building. She never saw the ghost herself but recalled it used to manifest itself to many of the tenants and introduced itself as Lucille. Just visualize that ad. "Cozy apartment in historic section. Has hot and cold running ghost!"

Daytona even has its own mascot ghost. Brownie, The Town Dog, lived on Beach Street in the mid 1900's. He was so beloved by local residents that someone started a bank account to take care of his needs. When he died, the money in the account was used to purchase a plywood casket and headstone with a bronze plate to be mounted on his grave. He is buried in Riverfront Park almost directly across from the Halifax Historical Museum. From 1955 to 1970, there was a second Brownie, known as The Post Office Dog because his favorite spot was near the Post Office.

Kathleen Walls

There are some that claim the original Brownie has never relinquished his watch over his favorite area of town. Perhaps if you visit the park after dark, you may be one of the favored ones to pet the spirit of this ethereal pooch.

Speaking of caskets, another of Daytona's otherworldly inhabitants was once a casket maker who lived above a furniture store on Beach Street. Today, it's a jewelry store. He was quite fond of spirits of a different kind and spent much of his afternoons in a favored haunt of his own, the local bar. So that his "bar time" was not a waste, he used the empty bottles to puff out the ruffled edges of the coffin's upholstery fabric.

To make up for lost time, he often worked in the early morning hours, tap, tap tapping as he positioned the used bottles within the fabric. To get the coffins out of the upstairs shop, he would slide them down a shoot to the ground. This made a terrible screeching noise as the nails rubbed the chute.

Evidently he had some premonition his heavy drinking was going to rush him into the hereafter prematurely. One morning, the storeowners didn't hear his busy hammer at work upstairs so they went to check on him and found him dead inside one of his own coffins. To this day, if you are on Beach Street in the early morning hours and hear a tapping followed by a loud screech, it's only the lonely coffin maker delivering one of his products.

Even the Orange Avenue Bridge leading to the Old Daytona section claims an ectoplasmic inhabitant. Many motorists have seen a dark haired woman near the approach to the bridge. Objects as large as chairs sometimes are tossed into the air even when there is no wind blowing.

Whether you spot Marian or any of the other ghosts in the area, the Riverfront Marketplace demands a visit if you want to understand the Old Daytona Beach that flourished before Bike Week and Daytona 500 became the national image of Daytona Beach. The entire area is charmingly restored and houses countless boutiques, antique shops, restaurants, nightclubs and the Seaside Music Theater, the area's only professional theater.

If you're looking for fresh fruit and veggies to munch as you ghost hunt, there is a Farmers Market held every Saturday on City Island near the Orange Avenue Bridge.

The Daytona Playhouse is another Daytona "hot spot" for other worldly players. I spoke with Artistic and Technical Director, John Stenko. He told of two actors whose ashes rest beneath the stage. One of them, Allan, is very active in the theater still. The other one, Doc, doesn't manifest himself often. John recalls several times when strange events occurred on or near the stage. "It was during a performance of *Dracula*. The director had rigged a large fake bat on a string that was supposed to swoop across the stage. We nicknamed it 'Binkey' but it didn't work very well and he finally gave up on it. Then during one performance, two other people and myself were on stage. Right on cue, this large bat flew across the stage. After the performance, I commented to the director, 'Binkey flew tonight, huh?' He replied, 'No, Binkey didn't fly.' Well, something flew across that stage we all saw it." Perhaps Allan found himself a bit part.

Another incident that occurred was in a small back dressing room that is also used as a snack room. John remembered, "One woman went back to get the

Finding Florida's Phantoms

coffee pot. She brought it out to fill up and when she returned to the break room, all the sugar packets were thrown on the floor."

I asked if he had ever seen the ghost. He pointed out some black short curtains called "legs" that could be moved around the stage. He recalled that a musical was the production that night. He was on stage and could see the back stage door from his position. "The door opened and I saw a figure of a man enter. When I went back to see whom it was, no one was there. No 'person' had entered that door."

John also spoke of other another spirit believed to inhabit the theater. "Before the theater was built, there was a home here. It was in the 1920's or 30's. A young woman lived there. Her lover left to go overseas and was killed. The woman - her name was Alice - was pregnant. One night, she drowned herself in the Halifax River just out back."

He believes she is responsible for some of the strange activities that happen there such as when the lights are turned off, only half go out. They are all on the same switch and there is no way some could be on when others are off. Also, the sudden chills commonly accompanying this type of phenomena are very present here. The signs in the lobby warn everyone to bring a sweater because the theater may become cold in some spots.

Some of the area's ghosts have been around a long time. Just north of the city in Ormond Beach, there is a prehistoric Timacuan Indian mound. It is believed that between 150 and 200 Indians are buried there. By day, it looks like just another pretty park with the river in the background but at night, well, many people won't go near it. If you're feeling brave, it's located on Mound Ave. and S. Beach. But remember this land was their land before sun, surf and fast tracks made "Daytona" a household word.

During the many centuries the Timacuans lived in the area, there were bound to be some tragic love stories. One such tale involves a young warrior who fell in love with the chief of a neighboring tribe's daughter. His father forbade him to see her, but like young people the world over, he was determined. He snuck away from the safety of the tribal fires with only his pine lighter torch to guide him as he sought his princess. It is said he was lost forever in what was then a vast wilderness near what is now the Tomoka State Park.

For years drivers heading north on Beach Street towards the park have reported strange lights that flicker among the moss draped oak trees on the side of the road. Skeptics try to explain the lights as swamp gas or a phosphoresce caused by algae, but there are others who swear it is the young brave still searching for his love.

If you plan to camp in the area, Tomoka State Park offers you an opportunity to stay where Native Americans lived long before the advent of the white settlers. You may or may not find ancient spirits wandering the shell middens along the banks of the Halifax Basin but you will find a picturesque spot among the oaks dripping with Spanish moss to park your RV or pitch your tent. Just don't go wandering off following any strange lights.

To glimpse the lifestyles of sea dwelling creatures, be sure to visit the Marine Science Center. A featured exhibit centers around the Sea Turtles. These ancient creatures are threatened with extinction as man invades more and more Florida beaches to build homes and businesses. Ask about the Ghost Crab.

Kathleen Walls

The Ponce Inlet Lighthouse may not harbor any ghosts that I was able to locate but it certainly has a colorful history and deserves a visit when you are in the area. Built in 1887, it has maintained its lonely vigil as a working lighthouse until 1970 when the Coast Guard Station abandoned it in favor of a new light on the south side of the inlet. The site has been renovated and houses museums in its three keeper's houses.

The area leading into the state's tallest lighthouse abounds in seafood restaurants. It's hard to make a bad choice here. The seafood is fresh and many offer waterfront dining from casual to downright rustic.

Another old site in the Daytona area that ought to have a few restless spirits, based on its history, is the Old Budlow Plantation and Sugar Mill. In 1821, it was the site of the town of Budlowville. During the second Seminole War, the plantation owner, John Budlow, sided with the Indians. When the Saint Augustine Militia captured the plantation in 1836 and forced John to accompany them, the Seminoles thought they had been betrayed and burned the entire town. The ruins of the plantation and sugar mill are worth a visit.

Far a different look at life in an early Florida community, visit Pioneer Settlement for the Creative Arts. Here you will find exhibits of folk crafts and skills that were necessary to survive in an earlier time.

For an introduction to culture that kids of all ages will love, visit the Museum of Arts and Science. From the natural history exhibit to the Planetarium, everyone will find something to enjoy.

One of Daytona's newest tours is sure to appeal. Haunts of the World's Most Famous Beach offers tours led by accredited ghost hunters. "Dusty" Smith, the tour owner, combines her knowledge of the paranormal with the history and legends of Daytona. They offer walking tours as well as a cruise tour.

Food is a necessity for those of us on this side of life's veil. Daytona has far too many great eateries to mention all but there are a few which are really unusual. The Dancing Avocado Kitchen in Riverside's Restaurant Row is a great place to stop for breakfast or lunch. It features an almost vegetarian menu but does offer some delicious burgers. Some items are unique like Cactus Salsa. It's sweet and just a little tangy. Of course, avocados are featured in many of the dishes such as Avocado Ruben's and Avocado Symphony Salad but they have lots of other delicious foods. For the diet or health conscious, this is the place. Chef Mario uses Canola Oil for frying. You can even get a side of non-fat sour cream for your quesadillos or nachos. They feature a large selection of non-meat burgers and great fruit smoothies as well as fresh fruit juice. Mario Steinberger and wife Angela operate the restaurant as a no-smoking zone. They try to offer healthy options when it comes to your dining. To the Steinbergers, the bottles artfully displayed over their door represent you the customer. They feel. "The bottles vary by size, shape, color, age and origin. They are similar yet different, but all are created fragile vessels."

For more upscale dining, try Martini's just down the street. Reminiscent of a Manhattan club, the food is international, the decor is plush and the lounge is jumping.

To find out if "everyone" is correct, try Aunt Catfish's. It has been voted the best dining in the Daytona Beach Area for 2002. You can dine on the water or

Finding Florida's Phantoms

even book an eco-cruise that departs from their dock. Seafood is my choice there but they have a huge menu designed to please all. Sunday Brunch is a special treat.

The Pinewood Cemetery is reputed to be one of the most haunted cemeteries in America. Just across the street, you will find a famous haunt of a different kind, Boot Hill Saloon. The walls are covered with memorabilia gathered over the last 30 years since Boot Hill became a cornerstone of Bike Week events. It's a classic first stop for bikers arriving in Daytona. Boot Hill welcomes all; business men as well as bikers fill its stools. There are rumors that many of Pinewood's residents still frequent their friendly neighborhood bar. Boot Hill Saloon's motto, "Order a drink and have a seat. You're better off here than across the street," applies to any of their clientele.

Daytona Beach is a place practically designed for the tourist. It is impossible to include every worthwhile experience in the area. Of course, it is most famous for its beaches and auto racing. It is probably the most biker friendly community in the world. It's also one of the most popular Spring Break spots. If you are not interested in any of these things, Daytona Beach will be more enjoyable for you when Bike Week, Spring Break or the Daytona 500 is not in full swing. I have listed a calendar of Daytona Beach's major festivals and events to help you plan a very spirited trip.

SPEEDWEEKS
January - February
http://www.daytonaintlspeedway.com
BIKE WEEK
February - March
February - March
http://www.officialbikeweek.com
SPRING BREAK
March
SPRING DAYTONA BEACH CAR SHOW AND SWAP MEET
March
http://www.carshows.org
BLACK COLLEGE REUNION
March
http://www.blackfloridian.com
PEPSI 400
July
http://www.daytonaintlspeedway.com
FLORIDA INTERNATIONAL FESTIVAL
July
http://www.fif-lso.org
October
http://www.biketoberfest.org
HALIFAX ART FESTIVAL
November0
(800) 854-1234

DAYTONA TURKEY RUN
 November
http://www.carshows.org
BIRTHPLACE OF SPEED CELEBRATION
 November
(386) 677-3454
www.ormondchamber.com

Contacts:

Daytona Beach CVB
www.daytonabeach.com
800-854-1234

Marine Science Center
www.marinesciencecenter.com
386-304-5545

Halifax Historical Museum
www.halifaxhistorical.org
386-255-6976

Daytona Playhouse
386-255-2431

Bulow or Tomoka S. P.
www.dep.state.fl.us/parks
386-676-4050

Ponce Inlet Lighthouse
www.ponceinlet.org
386-761-1821

Ghost Tours
www.hauntsofdaytona.com
386-253-6034

The Museum of Arts and Sciences
www.moas.org
386-255-0285

Aunt Catfish's
yp.bellsouth.com/sites/auntcatfishesontheriver
386-761-2744

Dancing Avocado Kitchen
386-947-2022

Cassadaga

As I researched this book, I found that most people look at you strangely when you walked in and asked, "Got any ghosts here?"

Not so in Cassadaga. Other than preferring the word "spirits" to "ghosts," they are more than happy to talk about their otherworldly guests. To understand the reason, you just need to look at the history of the picturesque community in South Central Florida.

Cassadaga was founded by George Colby. He was a spiritualist from New York. George suffered from tuberculoses as a young man. He was seeking healing as well as spiritual fulfillment when he was told at a séance that he was destined to found a Spiritualist community in the South. In 1875, George followed that dream and was led by Seneca, his spirit guide, to a beautiful hilly area not far from present day Orlando. He homesteaded the land and, in 1895, deeded over 35 acres to the newly incorporated Cassadaga Spiritualist Camp Meeting Association. The name means "rocks beneath the water."

The new community was especially powerful since it was believed to be a geomagnetic vortex, a place where psychic energy is concentrated. Over the years, the tiny community has thrived and is now the home for many of Florida's best-known mediums. For people with a mediumistic gift, Cassadaga is *the* place to live. Where their lifestyle is mocked in many places, here it is not only accepted but reverenced; where they are considered "different" other places, here they are the norm. As some towns grew up around a local industry, so has Cassadaga. Most of the town is dedicated to Spiritualism.

The hub of Cassadaga is the hotel. Worth a visit just for its architectural splendor, the hotel is listed on The National Register of Historic Places.

Carol Taylor works at Cassadaga Hotel. She is a natural medium. As a child she would see "people walking around" that weren't physically there. At first, she thought everyone saw these things. Later as she grew older, her gift terrified her and she consciously tried to shut down.

When she came to Cassadaga, she understood her talent and began to once more open herself up to these experiences. She now had the help to understand the difference between the good and bad energies and spirits and learned to protect herself from the negative ones while helping to convey the messages from the others.

When I asked her, "How many spirits reside at the hotel?" she laughed. "Many." She began with Arthur, one of the better-known ones.

"He was like an old fashioned clerk at the hotel. That is how he presents himself to me. Silver gray hair, starched white shirt, dress pants, vest and he likes to smoke his cigar. He likes to stand at the top of the staircase and watch over things. Sometimes he hangs around rooms 17 and 18." She smiled as if recalling her favorite things about a cherished old uncle.

"He's a prankster. Sometimes when the girls are giving readings, he will go in and throw out information he is not supposed to. The girls will chase him out again."

"Have you actually seen any spirits?" I queried. A pretty silly question to put to a woman who had already told me of her psychic history.

She nodded, "But my first encounters were with two little girls, Sarah and Caitlin. I started out here as a housekeeper. Sarah is about five or six, blond curly hair, dressed in turn of the century style clothes. Caitlin and Sarah both died of consumption. They aren't related or even from the same era. It's just children are drawn to other children. They love to play. Sometime they like to run their fingers through a person's hair. You'll feel a little vibration from them. They don't want to be forgotten. They sometimes play with the fans and turn them when they are off. Often people will be in their room and see a little girl peep around the corner. They will come to me and say, 'There is a child in my room but I had the doors locked!' They didn't realize what they were seeing."

She talked about the fact that living children seem to be a magnet for those who have "passed on." "They love their energy. Another thing is children aren't afraid of them. They just accept it as natural."

She went on, "Diane's little granddaughter was raised with them. They used to play together. They lived here for a long time and just moved out a little while ago. They didn't like that. It was like, 'You took the baby away.' They have gotten quite active lately. Mischievous things like we had some ladies talking to me at the front desk and all of a sudden all of the books on a shelf will go on the floor. Like a hand swiped them. The ladies looked at me like, 'I didn't do it!' The look on their faces was like, 'I guess I should have bought a book. Yes. I had better buy a book!'"

The girls aren't the only spirits at the hotel, not by a long shot. "We have Jack. He used to live just down the street. He always wore a dark brown suit and that is what we see him wearing now. He just died about three years ago and he

Finding Florida's Phantoms

hasn't passed on to the other side yet. He used to come here to have lunch. He still comes here and smokes his pipe on the porch. A little eight year old boy saw him last week."

At the time, Carol had a very bad chest cold verging on phenomena The boy came over to her and said, "You have a black chest" She asked him, "Do you know what you are seeing?" he shook his head. She explained that he was seeing her aura. She asked his mother about the child's gift and the mother told her, "He sees deceased people all the time." So I told her to take him for a walk around the hotel and see who else he sees. When they came back, the boy said, "I saw an older gentleman in a dark brown suit upstairs." She explained "That's Jack."

She recalled, "That child looked so relieved. It was like, 'Finally! Someone understands.'"

Carol remembers her own youth and hopes the little boy's parents help him learn to accept his gift. "I had a long talk with the mother and told her that her son has a fabulous gift. He can be a great healer. You should nurture this gift and help him understand it. I wish I was given the opportunity of parents who knew more about it and helped me nurture it but I didn't. I had to go the other way."

"We also have Mary. It was a home for the aged once upon a time. It was leased out. She likes it around room 5."

She explained that many different paranormal groups have been here and captured lots of orbs in the hallways near that room. Sometimes, she has the investigators walk down the hall one by one to see how sensitive they are. One young man was near the door to room 5 and he stopped and clutched his chest. She asked him, "What are you feeling? That's Mary; she died of a heart attack in that room."

She continued, "We also have a spirit I call 'The lady in White.' She looks like a schoolmarm, light brown hair up in a bun and a starched white dress. There is Henry. The first time I encountered him, he startled me. I was working late in the café (Lost in Time Café is the hotel's own quaint dining spot) and suddenly I saw this man in a long monk's robe. He startled me but as I got to know him better, I realized he was just sad. He was from the time of the aged home. He was deformed and his family sent him here to die. He could pass over but he just won't. He is quite harmless. He just wants someone to talk to. John is a tall spirit who was also there in the aged home. He is very proper and prim. If he didn't like the people in room 10 the night before, he ties the curtains in a perfect knot. It is like the knot is exactly the same all across the room. Perfectly knotted as if they were measured."

There is another religious spirit that stays at the hotel, Victoria the nun. Carol feels that the two spirit children, Sarah and Caitlin, see her as a mother figure. "Sometimes, I open a room door and there is Victoria with the two children clinging to her habit. I just back out, close the door and say, 'Excuse me.' I have respect for them and I feel they feel the same about me. Believe me, if they didn't, they could run me off easily."

I asked if she had any idea of Victoria's era. She wasn't sure. The original hotel burned down in 1926 and destroyed all the records. It was rebuilt in 1926.

Sometimes ghosts don't stay put. Carol told me of a case where a spirit child followed a living one home. "His name is Jimmy and here is what happened.

Once, we had a family in here. They had a cute little baby girl. They talked to me a while and then left. That evening as I was shutting up, the mother came banging on the door. 'Something is wrong with my baby,' she was screaming, almost hysterical. I got her calmed down some and asked why she thought that there was a problem with her baby. She told me 'She is always a good baby. All the way going home, she kept looking like she was staring at something we could not see. Then when we put her down for bed, she kept saying 'Jimmy, no. No, Jimmy.' And wiggling her toes around.' I realized what had happened. Jimmy, one of our spirits, had followed the baby home. I told her to go home and tell him he had to leave. He could come back here or somewhere else in the camp but he could not stay at her house. I guess he did since I never heard anymore from her."

A strange thing happened to me during my interview with Carol. My batteries went dead. Not an unusual occurrence you night think except for the fact that I had only used them for a few minutes and in the past I was able use them much, much longer without them going dead. Also, when I put in a second set, they were mysteriously dead as well. Luckily, the third set lasted until I finished the interview. I had charged them all just before I went to the hotel and have no "logical" explanation for what happened.

After the interview, I continued on my trip. When I got home, I had a call from Carol waiting on my machine. She felt she needed to tell me the "rest of the story."

According to her, there is one malevolent spirit still around the hotel. He is known to push or pinch women and has a dark feel about him. In researching, she found that at one time there was a man who lived there who was believed to have murdered three wives. No one ever knew for sure, but the one woman had died from a fall down the stairs. It was rumored that he had pushed her. Carol feels that this might be the same spirit.

The hotel is literally the heart of this placid place. It is an island of tranquility in a hustle bustle world. Carol said she felt like she came home when she moved to Cassadaga. Perhaps when you visit it, you will feel the same way.

Contacts:

Cassadaga Hotel
355 Cassadaga Rd.
Cassadaga. Fl 32706
(386) 228-2323
http://www.cassadagahotel.com

Carol Taylor
http://www.cassadagahotel.com/html/carol.html

Thirteen

Brevard County, Florida's Space Coast

Since the early days of the space program, Brevard County has become known as the Space Coast. Scenes of the VAB (Vertical Assembly Building) and the launch pads are recognized world wide since they have been on everyone's television screens. However, there is so much more to the county.

It is divided into North, Central and South Brevard and each section have distinct personalities and their very own ghost stories. Titusville is the main city of North Brevard, Melbourne is the chief city in the south and Cocoa, Rockledge and Merritt Island comprise the central section.

Titusville

Titusville was originally founded by Colonel Henry T. Titus. He was somewhat of a character and was known to sit on the balcony of the hotel he and his wife ran, Titus House, with a gun across his lap. However, he was never known to use it on anyone. He donated large parcels of land for civic use and was the person most responsible for having Titusville named the county seat of Brevard County.

He wrote, "Titusville is the grand center of all trade and will so continue to be. Her motto is to live and let live." Just four days later, on Sunday, August 7, 1881, Colonel Titus died.

His hotel later became the Dixie Hotel, which burned in 1962. The Federal Housing and Urban Development Building, Titusville Towers, now sets on the site.

Speaking of "Dixie," one experience you don't want to miss while you are in Titusville is eating Rock Shrimp at the Dixie Crossroads. Trust me! It's a culinary adventure.

One of the favorite things to do in Titusville is take the tour of the Space Center. Yes, it is a great tour. You will be brought into restricted areas. The museum displays real spacecraft from the past to present. The tour offers you a view of a simulated launch from a firing room where you witness a simulated Apollo launch. You get a feeling what life is like on the International Space Station. You may actually meet a real astronaut. The IMAX Theater shows a terrific film, *The Dream is Still Alive*. You even go out to the actual launch pads and the Complex 39 Observation Gantry.

There is one place they do not take you, a now unused Apollo launch pad complex. This place is the scene of some strange occurrences and some people believe it is haunted by the ghosts of the three Apollo astronauts who died in a fire here in the early days of the Apollo Project. Screams have been reported and the entire area will give you a creepy feeling if you are there at night.

The Emma Parrish Theatre is another Titusville location rumored to be haunted. The disturbances, strange noises in the empty building, are said to occur in the theater's attic. The cause of the haunting is not known but the facility used to be an old parking garage until it became the theater's permanent home.

The land surrounding the Space Center is part of the Merritt Island National Wildlife Preserve and includes land that was home to some old orange growers. Many people driving through the area have reported eerie happenings. However, even if nothing paranormal occurs, it is well worth exploring for its beauty and animal life. Endangered species such as loggerhead, leatherback and green turtles, the West Indian Manatee and more are located within the park.

Be sure to see the old Cape Canaveral Lighthouse. It is also on the Space Center property and can best be seen on one of the Center's tours. Only one story relating to any possible haunting there relates to a clock that flew off the wall in the 1800's.

Cocoa

When you visit Cocoa, the must see spot is the Village. This was once the main street with its hardware shop and Myrt's Diner. With the advent of malls, people stopped shopping there. In recent years, it has been restored with lots of art galleries, boutiques and great restaurants. It has a lovely little park named for former restaurateur, Myrt Tharpe, who went on to become the city mayor. Myrt's was a city landmark in the sixties. I remember once when I lived there going into Myrt's and having a sandwich with Jackie, a good friend. We were sitting and talking but the air conditioner was working full blast. I had a short-sleeved blouse on. Myrt noticed me shivering and came over and draped a sweater over my shoulders. "Keep this on until you leave, Honey. You look like you are freezing," Myrt commented.

I have shivered in vain in many an air-conditioned Florida business before and since but never had a response like Myrt's. She deserves her park and if by

Finding Florida's Phantoms

any chance her spirit is hanging around her beloved city, I hope if I ever see any spirit, it will be Myrt. I know she would be helpful.

One of the most dominating buildings on the Brevard Avenue is Cocoa Village Playhouse. Joe, the ghost of a former handyman, reportedly haunts the Playhouse. Footsteps are heard in the building when on one is walking there. Doors open and close by themselves.

A young actress who auditioned there claims she "heard whispers, and felt cold spots backstage." People frequently have the feeling they are being watched by an unseen spectator.

Built as the Aladdin Theatre in 1924, the Italian Renaissance style theatre was one of the finest theatres in the state. In the 1940's, it was renamed the State Theatre and showed movies.

The theater was built on the site of an old livery stable for the mule drawn wagons transporting supplies from the St. Johns River. Listed on the National Register of Historic Places, it has been restored to its original splendor.

Rockledge

Rockledge is one of Brevard County's oldest cities, incorporated in 1887 with only 150 residents. It was named for the long ledge of Coquina rock that stretches along the bank of the Indian River. Since then, people from all walks of life have been drawn to visit the small community. In its early days, many came by steamship and later by Henry Flagler's railway. Even President Grover Cleveland came to enjoy the sun and nearby beaches.

Most visitors came looking for fun or a healthier climate. Not all visitors had such innocent motives. One visitor brought death and a tragic haunting that persists to this day.

The tale centers around Ashley's Restaurant. It's a great place to enjoy a fine meal in atmospheric surroundings but sometimes the atmosphere is deadly.

It has had many incarnations. Built in 1930, it has been Jack's Tavern, Cooney's Tavern, Mad Duchess, The Loose Caboose, The Sparrow Hawk and Gentleman Jim's. Since 1985, it has been Ashley's. Through it all, at least one patron has remained loyal, the spirit of a young woman believed to have visited the establishment shortly before her brutal murder, Ethyl Allan.

Greg Palmer, the owner, showed me a picture taken on New Year's Eve 1998. The photo shows a distinct trail of "energy" around the bartender and the two people posing with him. He tells of his experiences in the restaurant. "You will be sitting at the bar and it sounds like someone clacking salt and pepper shakers together upstairs when no on is up there. Weird things, like once my wife was walking down the stairs and felt someone tapping her on the shoulder all the way down the stairs."

Greg tells of the many physics that have visited Ashley's. "One, Jean Stevens, reported seeing a woman killed going down the stairs to the lady's room. The apparition and her phantom boyfriend were arguing. He chased her down the steps, stabbing her, and finished killing her in the storage room near the lady's rest room."

Greg had many strange incidents almost from day one. He bought the place in November of 1985. One morning in January of '86, a strange looking man came to the restaurant. He claimed to be a physic from California. "There were five other people sitting around the bar while the man discussed his plans to do an exorcism. Myself, my wife, a woman named Barbara, the bartender, also named Barbara, and a waitress. This was all new to us; we had just taken over and we all got a kick out of this sort of thing. The physic claimed, 'Even as we sit here, I sense the presence of two more beings'. Strangely enough, my wife was only about four weeks pregnant and Barbara, the bartender, was also pregnant but she didn't even know yet. The guy never came back to perform his exorcism. We never saw him again.

"Another strange incident, I was working in the kitchen with a guy named Bob. And all of a sudden, the fan switches came on. I looked at Bob. He looked at me. 'Maybe they're halfway up?' But how often would two switches be halfway up? Neither of us was near them."

Ashley's is also reputed to harbor two other spirits. I asked Greg about this. He replied, "Actually there are three spirits. Gannett Newspapers hired physics to come in here, a while back. They determined that a twelve-year-old girl was killed by a car out front. She is here. Also, there was a man who worked around the place. He kind of worked for drinks. One night he got drunk, went out back, fell asleep on the railroad tracks, and was beheaded by a train. Because the original spirit was here, the others stayed too. Spirits attract spirits. That's what I've been told. If you look at the photos downstairs, there are three tracks." (When you visit Ashley's be sure to look at the photos located downstairs near the lady's rest room.)

Without a doubt, it is Ethyl Allan's restless spirit that is the centerpiece of the phenomena that occur in Ashley's and has been witnessed by owners, employees, guests and even local policemen. Police have responded to burglar alarms going off for no reason, women's screams when the building is unoccupied by any corporeal beings, and lights flashing off and on in the dead of night.

Ethyl's murder was probably the most brutal in the history of Brevard County. Ethyl was last seen in the company of a man who called himself Jim Wilson. Several friends saw Ethyl with Wilson on the night of Nov 18th, a Saturday. Ethyl visited a friend, Bill Sheeley, who worked in a packing plant, about 3 o'clock Sunday morning. According to reports in the Cocoa Tribune in Nov. 1934, "She told him she was going to Wachula where her mother lived with her brother, Jimmy, saying, it is reported, 'Now don't be jealous, it is only my brother.' She had no brother named Jimmy."

Wilson was a shadowy character. He had arrived in Rockledge about a month prior to the murder and rented a house on Barton Ave. just around the corner from the restaurant then called "Jack's Tavern". Other than a physical description, all that is known about him is that he occupied the rented house with a woman and a young man, believed to be his wife and son. For the last few days prior to the murder, he was alone at the house. He drove a Ford sedan with a Pennsylvania license. No one had ever taken down the number. He and Ethyl were seen in

Jack's the night of her murder. A neighbor reported seeing him packing his car on the day Ethyl's body was found.

Ethyl's badly mutilated, nude body was found by a passersby on the banks of the Indian River in Eau Gallie. Her throat had been slashed. The side of her head had been crushed and her upper teeth and part of her jawbone was missing. One leg had been almost severed. The body had also been burned and repeatedly stabbed. Identification was made by means of an unusual tattoo on the corpse's right thigh. It was a rope circle enclosing the initials "B. K". Ethyl also wore her gold and ruby ring, proving the motive wasn't robbery.

The police searched the area where the body was found in an effort to determine where the girl was murdered. The Tribune reported, "Nothing was ever found that would give even the slightest clue to where she was murdered." They speculated as to whether she was killed in a car, "or was the girl killed in some house, with other people knowing what was done?"

Wilson fled the area and was never apprehended. Could he have killed her in Jack's and later disposed of the body in the river? To this day, no one has answered the question, "Who killed Ethyl Allen?" Is that why she roams Ashley's? Does she want only justice? Or is she trying to tell people what happened to her so many years age? Probably we will never know but one thing is sure. Something unnatural is present in Ashley's of Rockledge.

Merritt Island

Another spot where you may meet the long dead in person is the Georgiana Cemetery. This is a very old cemetery located in the oldest section of Merritt Island off South Tropical Trail on Crooked Mile Road. The oldest legible tombstone dates to the late 1800's. However, there are many that are broken and crumbled. It was believed to have been built on old Indian burying ground. People have reported spotting an arcane presence there.

Melbourne

Originally, this small community located on a natural harbor of the Indian River Lagoon was called "Crane Creek."

It came to be "Melbourne" literally by chance. A specific name was needed to establish a post office there. The first postmaster, John Hector, was an Englishman who had formerly lived in Melbourne, Australia. He had moved here to establish a general store and the post office was located in his store. However, he had a different choice for town name. Mrs. R.W. Goode was the one suggesting "Melbourne". To settle the matter, the citizens drew straws. The straw with the name Melbourne won.

If anyone ever doubted that a ghost will remain on a site even after the building is torn down, Miguel's Mexican Restaurant is proof.

Miguel's was once the home of a rich bootlegger called Doc Sloan. It was a fancy Mediterranean style house that, in its later years, had become Miguel's Mexican Restaurant. Recently it was torn down and a new CVS Pharmacy built on the site.

Doc Sloan built the house in 1926 as a home for his family. One of his children, a three-year-old girl named Cora, was playing with matches and was burned to death on the second floor.

Over the years, a lot of spooky things happened at Miguel's. People heard footsteps on the second floor when no one was on that floor. Many people reported hearing a child crying in the upstairs floor of the restaurant; again, no one would be there. Sometimes glasses flew off the bar when no one was near them. The chandeliers would sway when there was no breeze. Laura's father worked there. "I wish my father was still alive to talk to you. He saw something go floating across the kitchen and he quit on the spot."

Then the restaurant was torn down and a brand new building to house the CVS pharmacy went up in its place. Of course, the price paid was the loss of a beautiful historical structure exchanged for a bland cookie-cutter type building with no architectural, historical or any other type of significance. New building means no ghosts, right? No way!

Already people who work in the drug store are reporting strange phenomena there. Laura Justice, whose family has lived in the area all her life, has this to say about her experience. "I work at the new CVS. One of the shift managers said she could hear crying in the morning before anyone gets there. She went looking for the sound. Found nothing except once in a while, something falls off the shelf or our alarm on the swinging doors to the stock room will go off with no one around. I went to work this morning. I put my purse in my locker, which is the third down on the very left. I am only 5'6 so it's perfect. I took out my cell phone and called my husband. I accidentally locked my lock and I was doing the combo while I was talking with my husband and opened it. I put my cell phone in my locker in front of my purse. Anyway, when the other girl showed up, she came up front with my phone. She was asking why it was in her locker. It fell out when she opened it. Her locker is the very top one. It is too high for me. I would have to stretch to put it in there. (We do have to leave it unlocked when we leave so hers was unlocked.) How could a ghost take it from my locker and put it in hers? We both knew about the ghost and shook our heads, feeling a bit confused."

One other building, the Henegar Center, has a different ending to the same sad story of how to deal with old decaying buildings that should somehow be preserved for posterity.

When the deterioration of two historical buildings in downtown Melbourne threatened their loss forever, a group of dedicated citizens banded together to preserve history. They formed the Brevard Regional Arts Group (BRAG) to revive the treasured landmarks. Both buildings were former public schools and the Brevard County School System donated them to BRAG with the understanding that they would be transformation into cultural arts facilities.

The Henegar Center for the Arts was thus born, named for Ruth Henegar, a dedicated former principal for whom the original middle school was named in 1963.

BRAG raised over $2.5 million to renovate the main building. The result; in 1993 the beautiful and functional Henegar Center opened its doors.

The group got a little bonus. Jonathan came along with the building. He is a friendly spirit who moves props and makes noises. Some people have even seen him in the balcony area.

Finding Florida's Phantoms

The entire county provides visitors with a diverse playground that offers the best of two zones, temperate and subtropical. From the sun and surf of the beaches to the wilderness trails of its preserves, from treasures of the past like the old lighthouse to modern marvels like the Space Center, this county truly has it all.

Contacts:

Brevard tourism
www.brevardcounty.com/about_brevard/travel_tour.shtml

Kennedy Space center
(321) 452-212
Fax: (321) 452-3043

Kennedy Visitor Complex
(321) 449-4444
Fax: (321) 452-3043
www.kennedyspacecenter.com/

Brevard Zoo
8225 N. Wickham Road
Melbourne
www.brevardzoo.org/

Emma Parrish Theatre
301 Julia St.
Titusville.
(321) 268-1125.

Canaveral National Seashore
308 Julia Street
Titusville, FL 32796-3521
www.nps.gov/cana/index.htm

Dixie Crossroads
1475 Garden St.
Titusville, FL 32796-3269
(321) 268-5000
www.dixiecrossroads.org/
A great site provided by Dixie Crossroads listing activities in the area.
www.dixiecrossroads.org/activities.html

The Henegar Center for the Arts
625 E. New Haven Avenue
Melbourne, Florida 32901
(321) 723-8698
Fax: (321) 952-0267
arts@henegar.org

Orlando

The most reliable story about how Orlando got its name is that a soldier, named Orlando Reeves, during the 1835 Seminole War saw an Indian sneaking up on his post near present day Lake Eola and shouted a warning. He was killed by a barrage of arrows. After the war, his grateful comrades named the place Orlando and stayed to make it their home. It is only normal that a town that was named for a person who died a violent death in the area should have more than its fair share of haunts. Orlando doesn't disappoint in that regard.

Sadly, the city proper seems intent on tearing down its historical past to trade in on a plastic future. The old Woolworth Building downtown was demolished because it "costs too much to preserve." Did the building's spirits go peacefully to their next plane when the building went? They were reputed to be two children who perished in a fire in the building many years ago. Only time and the inhabitants of the modern building that takes its place will know. The old McCrory's went down, too. Hadn't heard about any spirits there but the history was sure present.

Church Street Station, in the not too distant past the hub of Orlando's nightlife, is no more. Former Church Street Station owner/developer Bob Snow once had his office in a refurbished caboose parked on the tracks. In the 1970's, it blossomed as the fun place to have a good time in "The City Beautiful." Thankfully the buildings are still there, filled with paranormal energy. The buildings here, some of Orlando's oldest, are now empty of human presences for the most part but the others are still there. Spirits of newborns babies murdered by their prostitute mothers who worked in the brothel that later housed the Station's famous Lili Marlene's, an upscale restaurant. Guests frequently would be entertained by the spirit of an old piano player who sometimes thumped the ivories of the restaurant's piano late at night. Some have even seen him hunched over the keys pounding out an old ragtime tune. Another phantom entertainer who inhabits the place was a more modern one, a can-can dancer who died as she was dressing for her performance at Rosie O'Grady's, another of the Station's mainstays. Perhaps there are even earlier souls around the deserted complex.

Finding Florida's Phantoms

While Orlando is tearing down its history hand over fist, one place is seeking to preserve the past. The Orange County History Center. Built in 1927, the former Orange County Courthouse preserves and catalogues bits and pieces of Central Florida history. It also has some ethereal baggage from its days as a court of law. For example, one of the desks preserved there was the one occupied by Ted Bundy at his trial. How can you spot the desk? It's easy; he carved his name in it.

It also has another holdover from its courthouse days, the spirit of a sad lonely little girl. Her name is Emily and she is believed to have died tragically due to being placed with neglectful foster parents. The courtroom was probably the last place she saw her own family. She is usually found in an upstairs juror's waiting room.

Of course, every city has one cemetery that is particularly haunted. Orlando's is The Rouse Road Cemetery near the Seminole County line. The cemetery and the nearby woods are the midnight domain of Benjamin Miles. He is usually seen in fall and winter wearing tan clothes of the 1840's. He was a settler who is buried there in an unmarked grave. He appears to be angry and dangerous. A chill in the air and the call of an owl is your warning that he is near.

The prize for the most ghosts present at one site would have to go the Titanic Exhibit, Ship of Dreams. The exhibit gives a whole new meaning to the words "Living Museum." It is a cross between a museum and a Disney attraction. It is masterfully done and worth a visit even if there were nothing paranormal happening at the site. The exhibit owners describe it as "The only full-scale Titanic room re-creations in existence, including her world-famous Grand Staircase. Over 200+ priceless artifacts and historic treasures from some of the most prestigious private collections in the world, many of them on display for the very first time."

Strange events have followed the Titanic since before its launch so it is not surprising that this exhibit also has some attached spirits. Precursors of its ill luck could be read in the happenings at Harland and Wolf's Belfast shipyards. Harried Northern Ireland Protestant workers were accused of sabotaging the ship by their Catholic counterparts. Proof was offered to those who saw things that way. Titanic's hull number 3909-04, if viewed backwards reads, "no POPE," if the protesting Catholic workers were to be believed.

A cock was said to have crowed at its departure, which was deemed an ill omen by superstitious sailors. And worst of all, the ship was not properly christened.

Women in turn-of-the-century clothing have been observed especially around a trunk located in the museum. The trunk was found floating near the wreck site in 1912 and is now on display near the end of the museum.

Even specific people have been sighted. One is William Stead, a journalist and photographer who had warned about the disaster in a prophetic letter written years before the ship was built. He still sailed on the fateful ship and was lost at sea. Another is a little girl believed to be the spirit of Catherine Johnston, a seven year old who went down with her family that day. Catherine has been known to tug on guest's clothing and toss objects around the gift shop. She seems to desire recognition because her antics cease when she is addressed by name.

As to whether these sighting are real spirits or just induced by the realistic atmosphere of the exhibit only time and some good psychic investigation will tell.

Kathleen Walls

Winter Park is one of the prettiest little towns around Orlando and one of the most artistically inclined so it is fitting that it's best known ghost be located a place devoted to the arts, The Annie Russell Theater at Rollins College. This is Florida's oldest university theater. The grand entrance, the red velvet seats, the ornately carved décor and the priceless artwork all contributes to creating an atmosphere of another time, an era when the play *was* the thing.

Annie Russell's entire artistic life revolved around the college and the theater that bears her name. It was dedicated in March of 1932. She directed her first play there, *Romeo and Juliet*, in April 1932. She dedicated her life to the theater. Her living quarters and office are preserved in the theater building.

Annie's last portrait hangs in the complex. It was done by Eugene Coleman in 1987 from a photograph and caught her role as founder and director of the theater well.

She has been sighted in balcony of "her" theater many times. She always sits in the second seat of the last row on the far left. So common are the occurrences it has come to be known as "Annie's chair." She always wears a lavender dress and is a gentle benevolent ghost, here to protect her theatre. She once said, "I only wish I could live long enough to see how famous it will be."

Her prediction has come true. The program at Rollins is considered one of the five best in the entire country.

There is a possibility that Annie shares her eternal abode with another less noble spirit, a janitor who hanged himself in the basement below the theater. This basement is known on campus as "The Trap." It lives up to its name. It's a dingy, dimly lit concrete basement under the theatre that would be enough to give one goose bumps even without the knowledge of the long dead workman.

One old haunted landmark in Winter Park is what used to be the Alabama Hotel. It is now a private home but probably still harbors the ghosts of the guests murdered on its opening night in 1922. It was operated as a hotel from its opening until 1979. Then was a condominium for a time. It sat empty for a while before being purchased by its present owner.

A Mr. Hakes noticed an unusual fruit growing on one of his trees that had been budded with budwood brought from Jamaica. He then showed it to Temple, who in turn showed it to M. E. Gillett of Buckeye Nurseries. They purchased the tree, and erected a padlocked fence around it. The nursery determined that it was a 50-50 cross between an orange and a tangerine, and budded thousands of new trees from it. That first Temple Orange tree is now believed to have more than 7 million descendants.

Just North of Orlando is the less hurried town of Maitland. Filled with lakes and parks, one spot stands out, The Maitland Art Center. The center was the dream of one man, Jules Andre Smith and many say he is still enjoying it.

Smith moved to Maitland in the early thirties. He designed sets for Annie Russell's productions and through her, met Mary Curtis Bok. Mrs. Bok was impressed with the artist and offered to donate money to fund a "laboratory studio to be devoted to research in modern art."

Smith directed the construction of this research studio carefully. In the end, it resembled an Aztec/Mayan walled garden. Some of the greatest artist of the day stayed and worked there.

Finding Florida's Phantoms

Today at the Maitland Art Center, Smith's presence is frequently felt by visiting artist. One artist, James Cook, heard two disembodied "people" critiquing his work. The male sprit, who he felt was Smith, made such profound comments concerning the piece that Cook made some drastic changes in the work. Afterwards, he felt the critique had given him insight into creating a vastly better creation.

Another artist glimpsed a transparent "Smith" as he was preparing to leave for the night. He locked up and got out in record time that night.

Many people have smelled cigar smoke of the type smoked by Smith even though the studio is a no-smoking area. Smoke is also smelled in the garden in the two favorite places where Smith used to meditate. Cold spots, rocking chairs and footsteps have also been recorded in the building. A particularly odd occurrence happened when one of Smith's own works was hung in the studio. A recorder left in the building on the auto mode picked up a thumping, stepping sound. This is particularly odd since Smith had a wooden leg and sometimes used a crutch, which would have made that same sound. The occurances are more pronounced from September to May. Perhaps because Smith always traveled in the summer.

Although Smith was buried in Connecticut, perhaps he made his intentions known in life when, referring to the art center, he proclaimed in his will. "I will always be a presence here."

Longwood is Seminole County's oldest city dating back to around 1876. It quickly became a thriving winter resort by the 1880s. Its historic district is almost hidden near the intersection of CR427 and SR 434 but it is worth hunting for.

Its first hotel, the Longwood Hotel, opened its doors in 1887 and attracted visitors from all over the United States. Today, the hotel has been converted to offices but its original residents persist in being heard. Witnesses have observed lights turn off and on by themselves, footsteps are heard but no one is there, the elevator is notorious for its "self operation." Police have been called in one morning about 2:30 am to check out a possible burglary there. The first officer on the scene spotted someone in a window. They set up a perimeter around the building and did a room-to-room search. No one was found.

Another Longwood hotspot is the Inside-Outside House (now home to a small business called Culinary Cottage). The history and unique architecture of the house deserve a look even if it had no haunting presence. In fact, this might be considered a precursor to the pre-fab homes that later became commonplace.

In 1870, Captain W. Pierce, a Boston sea captain, decided to build a home for himself, his wife and black cat Brutus. If it had remained near Boston, it still would be unique because the captain built it with the framing structure on the outside of the siding similar to shiplaps, thus the name "Inside-Out House."

However, Captain Pierce did what many others then and now do; he moved to Central Florida. What makes the captain's move so unusual was that he took his home with him. He had the building dismantled and sent by ship to Jacksonville, then barge to Sanford, then mule drawn wagons to Altamonte Springs, where it was used as a military way station as well as the captain's home. It was later moved by more by modern vehicles in 1973 to its present destination in Longwood.

Kathleen Walls

Today, it is home to the Culinary Cottage, a unique gift shop owned by Pamm and Jim Redditt. The Redditts are not eager to spread the tale of their ghostly captain and his spirit cat, but they did tell me that things happen in the store. One incident Jim recalls most vividly is that of a Victorian house that will not stay put. "It just keeps coming off the shelf."

Pamm has seen the silhouette of the captain staring at her sometimes but feels he is pleased with their use of the house and will never harm anyone. Since many people have spotted a black cat sitting in second story window where the captain lived when there are no real life cats there, it's pretty evident that Brutus has refused to be unseated from his favorite spot. Little things like the house moving around or death will not deter a determined cat. Anyone who had tried to make his or her cat do something it doesn't want to do understands this principle of cat philosophy well.

Other customers have felt a ghostly brushing against their legs as they browse in the store.

When you decide to grab a bite to eat, Chef Arthur's next to the Enzian Theater is the place for ghost hunters. The theater has been rumored to have a resident present but the theater management denies it completely. However, at Chef Arthur's it's a different story. The building housing it was built in 1921. Many strange incidents occurred in the restaurant. Most around the place where a fireplace had been once. Now it is hidden by a large cupboard.

Assistant Chef Garrott Dwight looked up one day and saw a figure standing in the restaurant. No one was supposed to be in the place since it had not yet opened. It just disappeared. "It really spooked me."

Chef Arthur showed me a place where you can feel a drastic temperature change between places just a few feet apart. There was no air conditioning duct to account for the difference and it isn't something that is always there. Another thing he attributes to the unseen presence is the disappearance of knives and other instrument. "They will be in their rightful place and then next time you look they are gone and just as suddenly they are back in place."

A bartender, Jessie, has very long hair and she often feels someone playing with strands of it. They will twirl it as if wrapping it around ghostly fingers.

As you drive into Orlando from the north near the I-4 bridge over the St. Johns River in Seminole County, you are passing over what is known as the "Dead Zone." This short quarter mile section of I-4 has chalked up more traffic accidents than any other section of the interstate. Cell phones often will not work in this section, and your car radios may pick up voices of the long dead. There have been reports of a hitchhiking ghost in the area.

Why is this spot so unusual? Over one hundred years ago, there was a settlement here called St. Joseph's Colony. When a Yellow Fever epidemic swept the colony, some of the dead were buried in a small cemetery under what is now the interstate. The dead bodies were never relocated before the highway was constructed.

The I-4 Dead Zone has been investigated by more than one psychic investigator and all have reported abnormal findings here. The Florida Department of Highways admits to the unusual high number of accidents but blames it on "a congested section of the highway." Some psychics consider this area where you actually drive over dead bodies to be the most haunted place in Central Florida.

Finding Florida's Phantoms

Orlando and its surrounding areas are filled with ghostly presences. You just have to hunt a little harder to find them there.

Contacts:

Titanic-Ship of Dreams
8445 International Dr
Orlando, FL 32819
(407) 248-1166
www.titanicshipofdreams.com

Orange County History Center
65 East Central Boulevard,
Orlando, FL 32801
(407) 836-8591
exhibits@ocfl.net
http://www.thehistorycenter.org/exhibits.htm

Orlando Ghost Tour
(407) 992-1200
michaelgavin@orlandohauntings.com
http://www.orlandohauntings.com/

Chef Arthur's Restaurant & Tree-top Lounge
1300 S Orlando Ave, Maitland, FL 32751
(407) 647-7575

Longwood Historical Society
175 West Warren Ave.
Longwood, FL 32750
(407) 332-0225
www.ci.longwood.fl.us

Culinary Cottage
(407) 834-7220.

Annie Russell Theatre
Rollins College, Winter Park,
(407) 646-2145

Maitland Art Center
231 West Packwood Avenue
(407) 539-1198.
(http://www.maitartctr.org/).

Maitland Historical Society
http://www.maitlandhistory.com/exhibits.html

Kissimmee-St. Cloud

Walt Disney wasn't the first entrepreneur to realize the potential of this Central Florida area. In the spring of 1925, three businessmen arrived in St. Cloud. They were enthralled by the profusion of oranges, grapefruit and other citrus trees enfolding on the landscape as far as the eye could see. They decided to invest in the area. They, and a fourth partner, purchased almost the entire city block on New York Avenue. They decided the town needed a magnificent hotel.

Their vision resulted in the Hunter Arms Hotel. The Hunter Arms was ultra-modern for its time. It boasted a massive lobby with an exposed beam pecked cypress ceiling, Spanish tile floor, a pink Georgia marble office counter, a grand coquina rock fireplace and a private bath and a telephone in all the rooms and suites. Several shops were also housed in the hotel to accommodate guests.

The red brick Spanish Mission style building still dominates the historic district. It still has its antique phones in each room. It went through several incarnations over the years as it aged and was supplanted by newer more successful hotels. It became an "Old Folks Home" and then a bed and breakfast. In 1977, the present owners, Edward Minor and his sister Meredith, took it over and began renovation on it. It once again accommodates guests with, if not the modern elegance of the 1920's, the charm of days gone by. The gardens and lobby are often used for wedding receptions. However, over the years it has acquired something else, its own ghost.

At some point in its history, two sisters owned it. One of them, Vivian, died there. When the current owners began remodeling, a lot of strange things happened. Maids reported seeing an apparition in a white dress. They saw her so often they felt they needed to give her a name so they began calling her "Vivian."

The night manager, Bill Harris, related an event that happened shortly after that. "The manager then was Katherine Green. Once when she had some friends visiting, they were sitting on a couch in the lobby when the friend's little boy said, 'Mom, I have to go to the bathroom.' Katherine just directed him to the ladies room. The little boy came back and said, 'She won't let me in. She says that is for girls only.' The group all went into the ladies room. They saw no one. The little boy pointed. 'There she is.' Ask her what her name is Katherine told him. The child did, 'She says it's Vivian.'"

Finding Florida's Phantoms

Bill also tells about things disappearing. "I'm a culinary student so I do a lot of pastry cooking and I have a special place I keep my rolling pin. One day I looked for it and it was not there. Finally, I bought a new one. I stored it where I kept the old one. The next day when I went to get it, both of them were there." He shrugged, "Some rooms, 229 and 218, are particularly apt to experience phenomena. Women are usually visited more than men. During periods of remodeling, people see her more often."

Bill also informed me that some physics that visited the hotel told him that there are other spirits present besides Vivian. However, he commented, "She's the only one we have any contact with."

Vickie Mullin, the day manager, has never seen Vivian herself but she says many of the maids have seen her and guests often report things being moved around in their rooms.

Margie Payne the head housekeeper is a firm believer. She has seen Vivian walk past her in the hall. "Just a cold chill went over me. It was like a 'whoosh' went by me. She also gets in my housekeeping supplies and messes thing up."

A friend of hers, Mel, was in what was then a kitchen but is now a party supply store housed in the building. "Mel was working in there and the utensils began flying around. She actually took pictures of a smoky image. You can tell it's not cigarette smoke. It is too thick."

If you are looking for a clean moderately priced place to stay next time you visit Disney World, try the Hunter Arms. Some of its residents are out of this world.

If ghosts make you hungry and you don't want to stand in Disney lines for a burger, try the Silver Lining Café. It's in one of the original storefronts and is rumored to be visited by Vivian or one of her cohorts. Dean and Lynn Travett provide a different special every day.

A unique attraction in this area is the Cannery Museum. It is the only student run museum in the country. Mary Lee Powell's students at the Michigan Avenue School started the museum in 1992 to help preserve the history of Osceola County. It is located just down the street from the school. Rumors claim it is haunted.

While you're browsing Saint Cloud's historical district, be sure to check out the G. A. R. Museum dedicated to the Civil War soldiers that fought in the Grand Army of the Republic. Mount Peace Cemetery, also in the area, is always a good place to hunt for departed souls. It is the final resting place for more than 300 Civil War Union veterans and 2 Confederate soldiers.

The Magic Kingdom may have some "Light and Sound" activities going on that are not accomplished by high tech electronics. The Haunted Mansion is one of the most popular "dark" rides. Given that and its theme, it's only natural that many ghost stories have been told about it. Are any of them true? Who knows?

Two of the most commonly reported sightings there are of a man, sometimes with a cane, sometimes wearing a tuxedo. No building ever existed where the Haunted Mansion is now but there was a plane crash nearby. One man was killed and the rumor is that he is the man with the cane.

Another place where an apparition has been spotted repeatedly is near Cinderella's Castle. One possible explanation could lie with a murder in the late seventies. It was during the celebration of Mickey's fiftieth birthday and the park was drawing huge crowds. A young cast member who often portrayed Snow

White was abducted and killed. Her body was found not far from the Magic Kingdom. Could she be that sad hooded figure in brown?

Kissimmee is still known for its horsemen. The Silver Spurs Rodeo is held there yearly. However, ghost hunters might find a different kind of horseman, a dead one. Just south of town, there is an ancient moss draped oak tree called Dead Man's Oak. For over a hundred years, people have reported seeing a headless horseman riding a white horse near the oak. Legend claims he is the spirit of a man beheaded by Spanish soldiers beneath this tree centuries ago.

The historic center of Kissimmee is the Osceola County Courthouse. Dedicated May 6, 1890, it is listed on the National Register of Historic Places. Although I wasn't able to uncover any ghost stories connected with it, it is one of the state's oldest courthouses and the only courthouse in daily use since it opened.

Another Kissimmee museum where you can catch a glimpse of "Cracker Life" at the turn of the century is Osceola County Historical Museum & Pioneer Center.

Saddle Rack's Historic Walking Tour brings history to life to show a different era in Osceola County, one dominated by wild cattle, steamboats and the citrus industry.

Remember that Disney World and much of the surrounding area were once orange groves. Lots of things happened here that cannot be controlled by programmers and technicians. When you visit Mickey's next-door neighbors, be prepared for some noises in the night that may not be made by a mouse.

Contacts:

Walt Disney World
www.disneyworld.com

Hunter Arms Lodge
www.hunterarms.com
(407) 891-9855

G.A.R. Museum
(407) 892-6146

Medieval Life
kissimmee@medievaltimes.com
(800) 229-8300

Mount Peace Cemetery
(407) 957-7243

Osceola County Courthouse
(407) 343-2ASK

Osceola County Historical Museum & Pioneer Center
(407) 396-8644

Saddle Rack's Historic Walking Tour
mr.earl5364@aol.com
(407) 847-5364

Lake Wales

Lake Wales has one of the strangest natural, or unnatural depending on how you look at it, phenomena in the country. Aside from that, it is a refreshing change from the more commercialized areas. It still reflects the way Florida looked B.D. (Before Disney)

Spook Hill is a marvel that has to be seen to be believed. I tried it and did not believe my own eyes. Folklore and legend offer more questions than answers. One story is that riders carrying mail between the Florida coasts found their horses breathless on the downhill swing. Another legend claims it is the result of an Indian Chief's struggles with a bull alligator that causes the seeming suspension of the laws of gravity.

But whatever the reason, drivers now follow a one-way road, than stop at a white line. Under a banner touting S-P-O-O-K H-I-L-L, they put vehicles in neutral, hold their collective breath and appear to roll slowly up an incline.

Plenty of visitors have already placed a carpenter's level near the hill's halfway point and found an upward slope that cars apparently follow. But there are skeptics. "It's an illusion that it's uphill, when in fact you're going downhill," insists Jim Palmer, a doctoral student in geology at the University of South Florida in Tampa. Just because we're in Florida, he notes, "the laws of physics are not suspended."

Whatever, the reason, it is a very strange feeling to find yourself in a heavy RV in neutral gear and rapidly rolling up a steep (for Florida) hill. The community has embraced their particular phenomena. One school principal at Spook Hill Elementary School managed to get permission from Harvey Comics to use Casper the Friendly Ghost as the logo.

"Make you the world a bit better or more beautiful because you have lived in it." So said Edward William Bok, philanthropist, Pulitzer Prize winner and editor of Ladies' Home Journal at the dedication of his gardens in 1929. The garden and world famous tower that is his legacy to the American people does that and so much more. He donated it to the state of Florida in 1929 so that all could enjoy his famous gardens. The gardens were designed by landscape architect

Frederick Law Olmsted, Jr. You wander through thousands of flowering plants and shrubs and will probably encounter some small wild life. The squirrels think this is their personal playground so they scamper very close to the visitors.

The gardens sit atop Iron Mountain, one of Florida's highest points at 298 feet.

The striking simple architecture of the tower dominates the 128-acre botanical garden surrounding it. It rises another 205 feet. Designed by architect Milton B. Medary, it is built of Georgian marble and Florida coquina rock. Inside is 57-bell carillon that can be heard all over Lake Wales.

Pinewood Estates is a 20-room Mediterranean Revival historic mansion incorporated into the gardens. Tours are held daily so you can observe how the rich and famous lived during the gilded era. Originally named "El Retiro," meaning retreat in Spanish, the estate was built in the early 1930s for Charles Austin Buck. Buck made a fortune in steel and wanted a winter estate where he could relax with his family.

People still come to this small Florida town from all over the world to have the wrinkles of their soul ironed out by the awe-inspiring carillon music that wafts through the garden daily. Throughout the year, the gardens offer concerts of all different types.

There is so much more to Lake Wales, however, than the famous tower and gardens. This vintage town came into its own in the early years of the twentieth century with the Florida Land Boom. Its Historic District and Depot Museum preserves much of its heritage for you to enjoy, as well as a few resident spooks to mystify you. The brick depot covered with pink stucco with its red tile roof was built as a passenger station by the Atlantic Coast Line Railroad in 1928.

When passenger service ended in 1954, the depot was no longer needed. Then in 1974, the idea to turn the once beautiful building into museum to display the area's heritage developed. It opened in time for the nation's bicentennial and has been delighting visitors with its relics of yesteryear ever since. The museum also sponsors an annual Pioneer Day to celebrate Lake Wales' "Boom and Bust" days.

Aside from several permanent exhibits, it has many traveling ones that change regularly. Some things about the Depot never change, however. Two of the Depot docents, Fran and Jennifer, tell of some strange happenings in there. "We have little jokes, 'The ghost must have done it.' Things disappear. Not just little thing you might misplace. Items as large as a clothes steamer. There is no logical explanation for that."

Lake Kissimmee State Park also hosts a similar event, 1876 Cow Camp. South Central Florida was the heart of Florida cattle country at the turn of the century. The life of early Florida cow hunters is interpreted at the parks living history demonstration. In-character cow hunters and their herd of scrub cattle will give you a feeling of what life was like in a rough and tumble cow camp. The Cow Camp operates on weekends and holidays.

To understand the Lake Wales Historic District, you need to consider a bit of its history. It grew up in the early 1920's when money was easy and many people wanted to invest in the land of sunshine and orange groves. Then came the depression. Money was no longer plentiful but the city struggled to survive. Lately,

Finding Florida's Phantoms

it is experiencing a revival of visitors who want something more of a Florida vacation than man-made rides and crowds. The unique art galleries, boutiques, shops, and restaurants still retain their "Gilded Age" charm. In addition, murals telling the history of the city are now painted on many of the huge blank sides of the substantial buildings reminiscent of that era. On Fridays, a farmer's market springs up to offer the freshest of the area's produce.

When you visit Lake Wales today, you realize they have done much more than survive. They have thrived.

The Chateau Suzanne is another success story. When Bertha Hinshaw lost her young husband to pneumonia, she was devastated. Bertha and Carl had had great plans. They had formed a partnership with J. L. Kraft, of cheese fame, to build an exclusive community in central Florida on their pristine acreage. Before those plans could be executed, the great depression squashed the Florida Land Boom. Kraft withdrew. Those dreams were no linger feasible. Then suddenly Carl was gone. Bertha was left with limited funds and two young children to care for.

How often have a woman's dreams sprouted wings and taken on a life of their own? And how often have those dreams been spurred by necessity? It was 1931 and opportunities for women were limited. Bertha decided to do what she did best; she opened her home to paying guests. Little did she guess that she was beginning a venture that would make her inn a haven for travelers from all over the world. Her food has even traveled to the moon.

Today, Bertha's dream is in the safekeeping of another remarkable woman, Vita Hinshaw, Bertha's daughter-in-law. Vita's life unfolds like a movie script. She is a World War 11 WAVE who married her childhood sweetheart and now plays hostess to some of the world's most fascinating people as the chatelaine of one of the most romantic inns in America.

Chalet Suzanne has become one of the best-loved inns in central Florida. You don't have to be a jet setter to enjoy the lifestyle of the rich and famous here. Drop in anytime for a royal welcome. You can taste the famous Romaine Soup. One sip will tell you it truly is out of this world. You even visit the on-site cannery. Be sure to note the plaque that lists Chalet Suzanne as one of the NASA suppliers.

Another unique aspect of the Chalet is the bowl used for its signature soup. Resident artist and potter, Boz Birvis, pattern these wide-rimmed bowls after Norwegian ashtrays. Do stop by and watch Boz perform magic with clay.

Bertha loved beautiful things. She collected them on her travels like some women collect shoes. Her collection is preserved in a museum at the chalet, except for what is being put to use either on the grounds, in the restaurant or in one of the inn's unique rooms. Tiles and beautiful glass objects are all over the place. Perhaps, the ultimate magic behind this European style fairyland in the heart of Florida is that Bertha built her dream world for all to enjoy. Seventy plus years later, it's still making dreams come true for all who visit it.

Just to prove that the best things in life are free, Florida's Natural, a locally based citrus grower's co-op, offers you a chance to relax and have a free glass of ice cold OJ while you visit the Grove House. This is a reproduced cracker house that houses a small museum and theater dedicated to the growing of Florida's favorite crop.

Lake Wales certainly makes a Florida vacation trip more beautiful as well as more interesting, proving that Florida has more to offer than Disney.

Contacts:

Lake Kissimee Start Park 14248 Camp Mack Road
Lake Wales, Florida 33853
(863) 696-1112
1-800 326-3521 Camping res
no pets in campground
http://www.dep.state.fl.us/parks/district3/lakekissimmee/index.asp

Bok Tower and Gardens
1151 Tower Blvd.
Lake Wales, Florida 33853
United States
Tel: 941-676-1408
www.boktower.org/

Grove House
20160 US Highway 27
Lake Wales, Florida 33853-2425
863-679-4110
800-237-7805 x4110
10:00 AM - 5:00 PM Monday through Friday
10:00 AM - 2:00 PM Saturday (Seasonal)
Closed Sunday

Depot Lake Wales Museum and Cultural Center
325 S. Scenic Hwy. (U.S. Alt. 27), the museum is open Monday through Friday, 9 a.m. to 5 p.m., and Saturday from 10 a.m. to 4 p.m.

Chalet Suzanne
3800 Chalet Suzanne Drive
Lake Wales, FL 33859
800-433-6011

Sebring

As cities go, Sebring is a relatively new city, founded in 1911 by George Sebring. It is a city of contradictions. People usually move to Sebring for one of two reasons; either they are seeking peace and quiet or they are fans of sports car racing. The peaceful city, laid out by its founder in a circle around a lake, is home to the oldest and most prestigious road race in the country. It began on March 15, 1952, that first 12 Hours of Sebring race, and has been drawing the cream of the crop of the automotive racing world ever since.

Its founder never foresaw a sports event making the town famous. He envisioned a peaceful town where residents, all sedate Victorians, lived around the peaceful lake setting. In fact, at the unveiling of a bronze plaque placing the city's first hotel, The Kenilworth Lodge, on The National Register of Historic Places on January 26, 2001, Mr. Sebring (in the person of Bill Farmer) addressed the crowd regarding his intentions for "his" city. "When my family founded the enterprising city of Sebring, Ohio, we intended for it to become a great center for manufacturing in the Midwest. But my intentions for the Florida version of Sebring were to offer citizens a perfect opposite to the bustle of industrial endeavors. Only quiet, calm, and tranquil pursuits would occupy the residents of this lakeside retreat. The noiseless commerce of growing oranges would be the only manufacturing found here. Nothing was to disturb the health and happiness of the contented citizens of Sebring, Florida. Especially not the mischievous liquid of spirituous drink."

In many ways, George Sebring's dream has come true. Sebring is a delightful mix of athletes and retirees liberally sprinkled with pleasant small town people. In 1996, the town was designated a "Main Street Community." Much of the things that interest a visitor are in walking distance of one another: Sebring's Cultural Center that includes the public library, the Sebring Historical Society, Highlands Art League and Museum and the renown Highlands Little Theater..

The Kenilworth Lodge, which was built in 1916, has watched the city through all its cycle of boom or bust and is still the historic heart of Sebring.

When George Sebring and his contractor, B. A. Cope, designed the hotel, they planned the most modern facility possible at the time. He foresaw it down through the years sheltering the most illustrious visitors. It had indeed seen some big names under its roof. C.W. Nash, of the Nash automobile company, Adolph Ochs, owner and publisher of the New York Times, Colonel Lewis, inventor of the Lewis machine gun, and H.G. Hawk, the inventor of Post Toasties, have all stayed there. Perhaps the most impressive guest register was in 1924 when the National Governor's Convention, 42 governors and their entourage, stayed at the Kenilworth on a tour of the state.

The Kenilworth has some other more elusive guests. These guests never signed in and may never check out. Violet McGuire, the night manager, has had to calm down many of the people who came in contact with the hotel's ghosts. One man, Dwayne, was working on the third floor. He heard a tapping on the door and answered, "Come on in." No one did but the tapping continued, so he repeated the invitation. Finally, after the third round he got up and went to the door. He pulled it open irritably as the tapping went on. He was shocked to see that there was no one at the door. No one he could see anyway. He got downstairs fast.

Another workman, Ed, also on the third floor, was walking along and felt as if some invisible presence was trying to trip him. Knowing about the hotel ghost, he just stopped and gestured for "it" to pass him. Sure enough, he wasn't tripped again.

Violet also actually felt the presence herself on several occasions. Late one night, she was relaxing on the sofa watching an old black and white movie. She was caught up in the drama of the monsoon season in India when she heard someone enter and come over near the end of the sofa. She didn't look up, assuming it was Gordie, an older widower who often came in to pass the time with her at night. She felt him tickle her toes and shook his hand off, "Stop it Gordie, I'll talk to you after the movie is over," she told him. "After the movie ended I looked around for him and he was gone. I just figured he'd gotten tired of the movie and would be back later. Around six in the morning, Gordie came in and I asked 'Where'd you go?' He replied, 'What do you mean? I haven't been in here at all last night.' I was dumbfounded."

One morning, a man came down shouting that he wanted "out!" She said that was the first time she understood the expression "White as a sheet." He wouldn't say why he wanted to leave but she told him she could put him in another room but couldn't give back his money. He just said, "Never mind the money; I just want to get out." He never told her why but she had a pretty good idea.

Ghosts do not affect guests in the same way. One night, two women guests came down and told her, "There's a man floating around in the room." She just commented, "A good man is hard to find." The women laughed and went back to the room and apparently slept quite comfortably with their "guest."

Another guest, a local person who had sold his house, was staying on the third floor until he found more permanent quarters. He came down quite agitated one night and told her, "Something is tapping on my window!"

Violet replied, "It's probably just a bat."

He insisted, "No, there is a light there and I can see. Nothing is there. But after that, I saw this light in the room. I was so scared I put the covers over my head, then something was trying to pull them off of me. I was so scared I just hung on to those covers for dear life until it stopped."

Finding Florida's Phantoms

He checked out the next day.

The owners and employees call the ghost "Mr. Parker" after a former manager but Violet wasn't sure if that is in fact who it is.

Another employee, Kaylee Dawn Davis has seen "Mr. Parker." "He was just opening and closing a door on the third floor. He looked real, not like something you would see in a dream."

Another old resort that was built during Sebring's boom years of the 1920's was Harder Hall. The Biltmore's put together the financing for the $30 million dollar development, which was comprised of a major resort complex complete with its own golf course and home sites for residents that are more permanent.

But unlike Kenilworth's spirit, which is more mischievous than malicious, Harder Hall seemed to be under a curse. Near the end of the twenties, the Florida land bubble burst and Harder Hall changed hands many times. Most of its owners died violent or mysterious deaths. That seems to still be holding true. Its last owner, Avi Limor, a New Jersey investor who had purchased the property from the Resolution Trust Fund in 1994, was killed the following year in a plane crash. In addition, there were many accidents usually involving one or more fatalities.

Witnesses have seen lights, heard music and seen "people" either wandering around the ruined courtyard or peering out the windows of the abandoned building.

At this time, the fate of the hotel is in limbo. One developer, Marc Shenker, is willing to step up and take over. He has put his money where his mouth is. It just depends on whether the city fathers will decide to preserve this important, albeit ill-fated piece of history, for posterity or condemn it to the demolition ball. Personally, I hope Mr. Sheniker succeeds in his dream. He has the experience and the background to do it. I also hope he has lots of life insurance.

A visit to Sebring can be a peaceful experience relaxing in the sun and shopping in the quaint downtown shops. It can also be a frantically paced road race at the track. Whatever your pleasure, Sebring will oblige.

Contacts:

The Kenilworth Lodge
836 S.E. Lakeview Dr.
Sebring, Florida, U.S.A.
(863) 385-4686
mark@ct.net,madgekwl@strato.net

Top:Seven Sisters in Ocala
Photo by Kathleen Walls
Bottom: Halifax Historical Museum in Daytona Beach
Photo by Martin Walls

The ghost attracting wedding dress at Halifax Museum
Photo by Martin Walls

Top:"Lillian's Place." in Daytona Beach
Bottom: Carol Taylor shows the scene of a ghostly sighting, the bar at Cassadaga Hotel
Photos by Kathleen Walls

Finding Florida's Phantoms

Top: Chef Arthur's in Maitland
Bottom: Dr. Nassif shows off Annie Russell's portrait in her preserved apartment at the Annie Russell Theater
Photos by Kathleen Walls

Top: Hunter Arms in St. Cloud
Bottom: You can't see this one in person. It's Doc. Sloan's house now torn down to make way for a new CVS.
Photos by Kathleen Walls

Finding Florida's Phantoms

Top: An Apollo Rocket sits on its launch pad in 1967
Bottom: Ashley's of Rockledge
Photos by Kathleen Walls

Top: The Lounge at the Kennilworth Lodge
Bottom: A scene from the past at Lake Wales Depot Musuem.
Photos by Kathleen Walls

Eighteen

Southwest
Tampa Bay Area

Perhaps the pirates who left their legends in Tampa Bay were drawn by the same things that today draw millions of tourists to this area - fun, sun, sand and surf. Of course since the eighteenth century, Tampa has added lots of drawing cards to its deck. Attractions, restaurants, shopping, and countless other amenities designed to make a place an irresistible vacation destination has all added to Tampa Bay's appeal.

One other thing draws some more curious visitors - Tampa's haunted heritage. From health fanatics to actors, from businessmen to art students, Tampa has a fascinating stable of otherworldly residents.

Perhaps the best-known story concerns the Tampa Theater. Its history and architecture alone merit a visit but there is more lurking in its dark recesses.

The theatre was built by architect John Eberson in 1926 and has been a Tampa landmark ever since. The elaborate movie attracts over 150,000 people annually and is on the National Historic Registry. As you sit in the massive theater awaiting the lowering of the lights for a performance, you are surrounded by the atmosphere of a Mediterranean garden. After the lights go down, the starlit sky sparkles above. It was the masterpiece of its day when it opened. It even had air conditioning, which drew many people just for that in summer.

In a different twist on the *Phantom of The Opera*, Tampa Theater is rumored to be haunted by the friendly ghost of Foster Finley. Foster was the theatre's projectionist for 25 years until his death in the late 1960's. He would not leave the place where he had spent most of his adult life and is still glimpsed by visitors and employees alike.

He always came to work dressed in a suit, tie and hat and then changed in the dressing room. His nickname was "Fink." The new projectionist who replaced him did not last too long. According to Tara Schroeder, our guide, the poor man would hear the door open and close and no one would be there. At that time, the projectionist needed to switch from one projector to another one as the reels wound down. The toggle switch controlling this would be flipped before he could reach for it. The unnerved projectionist decided two projectionist in the small room was one too many, especially if the other one was dead. He quit.

Many of the theater employees heard keys rattling. On two occasions, two different employees who were opening the theater unlocked the door and entered then heard keys rattling at the level above the concession stand. They heard a key being put into the door up there and said, "Good morning." They then went up to see who was there only to find themselves all alone in the theater.

A group of St. Petersburg Ghost investigators came to the theater. They brought all the latest equipment and one that is still considered controversial, dousing rods. They tried to rule out any natural causes, for instance any wiring behind walls when the detectors went off. In some cases, the detectors would go off indicating energy at that spot. They would leave it and go back later and, if no energy was detected, ruled out wires since they would always be present. Tara relates, "At one place, I watched the meter go off and the temperature gauge dropped way down. Since it was so dramatic, they got out the dowsing rods. These were used to ask questions. If they crossed it indicated a 'yes.' They asked a few questions and nothing happened. I decided I would have some fun so I asked, 'Can I ask some questions?' I asked about several incidents like, 'Were you here when the keys jingled?' I asked, 'Were you employed here?' The rods crossed to indicate 'yes.' I went through the decades to determine the time frame. When I asked, 'Were you employed here in the 50's?' it indicated 'Yes.'"

Was Fink letting Tara know he was there and active?

Something about theaters seems to attract hauntings. The Faulk Theater has its departed actress, Betsy Snavely. Betsy hanged herself in a third floor dressing room sometime in the 1930's after her husband deserted her and ran off with a stagehand. The theater now belongs to the University.

Another theater in the area that boasts a resident haunt is the Lake Worth Playhouse. The art deco style theater began life in 1924 as the brainchild of brothers Clarence and Lucian Oakly. The brothers operated it as a combination movie palace and vaudeville theater.

The theater ran into some hard times. Vaudeville declined. A hurricane took off the Spanish style roof. Each time, the brothers coped. That is until June 30, 1931. Lucien blew out his brains on the back porch of his home. Incidentally, his insurance policy would have expired at midnight.

Exactly a year later, Clarence died suddenly.

After the brothers' deaths, strange incidents have been reported on into the present day. The theater changed its name in 1953 to the Lake Worth Playhouse but the shadowy residents continue to play tricks.

Toilet paper rolls will mysteriously be lined up in the lobby. Items as large as 5-gallon water coolers move around. Pictures of actors are turned to face the wall in the lobby. Footsteps echo from various places when there is no one in those places. One manager even reports hearing applause in the empty theater.

Physics have suggested exorcism but the current owners refuse. They feel their ghost is friendly and happy in the theater. When the last staff member leaves, he or she never fails to say, "Good night Mr. Oakley."

Perhaps it is an artistic temperament that causes souls to linger. In Brandon, just east of Tampa, a young art student has been seen. The only person who has seen her is Dick Cimino who has since passed away himself. However, before his death, he confided in others on the staff about the mysterious young girl dressed in blue. He believed her name is Matilda and she studied there years ago.

Some spirits are more intellectual and wouldn't be caught dead in a theater. Instead, they frequent the University of Tampa's Merle Kelce Library. You would think a library would be a strange place for a haunting with its rules about quiet but this library is definitely different. First, it's just down the street from the Tampa Hotel. Although the library is a stark modern building, the hotel, which now houses the Henry Plant Museum as well as offices and classrooms for the university, is a Victorian conception of an Arabian Nights fantasy. When Henry Plant built it in 1891, it was considered one of the largest and finest hotels in the country. It is reputed to have seen its share of spirit activity but the staff denies that it is haunted. Student reports are very different. They claim to have seen apparitions, felt cold spots and heard voices.

But the library? That is a different story. Kevin McGinn, Technical Assistant at the library, has had several unnerving experiences. The library is a relatively new building but that doesn't stop the spirits, associated with things that occurred there before the present structure, from causing disturbances. During the heyday of the hotel, this area contained a casino. It had a floor that opened and disclosed a swimming pool in the daytime and at night was closed to create a dance floor. Many celebrities visited and performed here then.

However, she said that the one visual experience she had was with a former employer. "He was behind me at the circulation desk. I think he pinched me one time. I have never seen him since but once when I was in the building with a friend after hours, we both had a strange experience. We had gone to a show and I had brought her back here to show her something. We were leaning over my desk looking at the papers. We both looked up at the same time and decided to leave. Neither of us said anything inside but when we got outside, she asked me, 'Did you feel someone pinch you?'"

The man in question as an employee who passed away in the seventies, Joe Figerota. He was only in his thirties when he dies. The library has a plaque on one of the pillars in his memory.

Kevin comes by her psychic senses naturally. She will tell you, "My mother is a sensitive and she has told me there are different types of energy here. Some good and some not so good. She has seen people in the stacks who appear as solid and you or me."

I asked if her mother had observed the clothing since that is one way to gauge the era the spirit might derive from. Indeed her mother had. One man was wearing a dark suit like those worn in the nineteenth century. This would coincide with the time the casino existed on this spot.

The library has some unusual objects in its collection. After all, how often do you find the ashes of a deceased benefactor in a library? Kevin looked upward and lowered her voice when she told of this. "There is a dark force here, too. It manifests itself mostly if you stay after hours. I don't stay after hours and work anymore. I had a terrible experience. The Special Collections is right up overhead." At that time, we actually heard a tapping that I was able to capture on my tape recorder.

Kevin shrugged it off as an everyday occurrence. "That's what they usually do. They know we're talking about them."

She continued to explain where she believed the "bad energy upstairs" emanated from, "The ashes of a descendent of one of the founders of Ybor City. They are there on the orders of a physic councilor. They are in a marble urn. The widow had a good bit of money and the pseudo psychic may have been trying to get some of it. My mother says he should not be here. His spirit is restless. His wife was also supposed to be interred here too but she is buried somewhere else."

At this point, I was not sure I wanted to accept her invitation to see the urns. The room is usually closed to the public but when we entered the deserted space surrounded by venerable old books, the feeling was similar to entering a mausoleum. The two urns stood next to one another and were the first thing anyone entering the room would see.

She described her "terrible experience" in that room as the feeling of being enveloped by a "psychic force"; a "disembodied evil" rather than a spirit of a departed person. "It was horrible! I felt an inhuman energy. Like one of the plagues of Egypt. Like when the death took the firstborn in a family."

Kevin also pointed out that there were also "good forces" in the room that seemed to try and counteract the evil. "Twice when I was working in here, I fell. Both times, I felt hands break my fall and lower me to the floor gently." She did not appear comfortable in the room and we left quickly.

The ladies room on the first floor is also haunted. She stopped in one night after work to retrieve something. Her mother and nephew were with her. As the building was dark, her mother said she was going to stay downstairs near the circulation desk. Kevin and her nephew went upstairs to the employee lounge to get some soft drinks. Meanwhile her mother went to the Ladies Room to wash her hands. While they were in the lounge, they received a frantic call from her mother, "She whispered, 'Get down here quick.' When we got to the first floor, she told us she heard singing in the Ladies Room, many voices, mostly female, and singing an operatic aria. The temperature in the entire area was dropping noticeably so we left quickly."

Others employees had strange experiences with that rest room. Two of them also heard the singing and a third just had a feeling of being watched when she was in the room.

Another possible explanation of the female singer is found in the story told by a former employee that a young woman committed suicide in the library. At that time, the library was located in the current Student Services building. Perhaps the woman moved into the new building when the library moved there. The death is believed to have occurred shortly after the university was built in 1956.

She frequently saw a phantom woman in the stacks on the forth floor near the special collections room after all the patrons had left the library.

Ybor City is a place no visitor to Tampa wants to miss. They come to see the museums reflecting the culture of another era. The nightlife and restaurants offer entertainment. Sometimes it is easy to forget that this hot spot for tourists was home for the thousands of emigrants who sought a better life in America at the turn of the century. Some still remain through the ages.

"To understand Ybor City, you must visit the clubs." At first, I took Helen Tasin's statement to mean nightclubs. But Helen, a representative of Centro Ybor, explained. In Tampa's historic Ybor City, "the clubs" have a whole new meaning.

Finding Florida's Phantoms

They represent a unique system the immigrants devised to survive in America's melting pot. Not only survive, but maintain their cultural identity.

Ybor City owes its existence to one man's dream. Don Vicente Martinez Ybor was a wealthy cigar factory owner in the latter part of the 19th century. He had moved his factories from Cuba to Key West because of labor unrest but found lack of transportation there a problem. Encouraged by Henry Plant's new rail line into Tampa, he brought his factories there. Other wealthy owners followed. The factory workers settled on the forty acres of Ybor City. Italians, Germans, Spanish, Jewish and other Europeans followed. Soon a thriving European community had sprung up on Florida's West Coast.

But Ybor City differed greatly from other enclaves of immigrants. The social clubs were one feature that made Tampa's cultural soup so appealing.

These "clubs" were the closest to our insurance polices that the immigrants had. As an immigrant in a foreign land, your life and culture revolved around the clubs from birth to death. For the nominal dues, you received a place to go to hear your native language spoken, an entertainment center, and hospitalization in sickness, health and burial insurance. Most importantly, the club dances and socials were a place your children would meet future spouses of "their own kind," thus hopefully insuring that their cultural heritage would not be abandoned by the second-generation immigrants.

El Circulo Cbano, as the Cuban Club was called, has at least one immigrant that is still clinging to the old ways. Dr. Paul Dorsal, a professor of History at the University of South Florida, tells of a piano-playing inhabitant at the club. "Several visitors have actually seen the keys moving and heard music when no living player was present."

The piano is located in the old dance hall of the club. The player is believed to be a young man who was killed near the club.

The public buildings are not the only place to retain long dead residents. Nor is the influx of immigrants looking for a better life totally over. One such immigrant is Shamus Hannigan. Both Shamus's face and his bar proudly display the map of Ireland.

The bar is up a dark flight of stairs. Within the James Joyce Pub, you might well be in the heart of old Erin. The only windows are to the front of the narrow building causing dark shadows throughout. The rich old wood of the long bar add to the feeling of twilight even at midday. But the bar was not always just a good place to escape South Florida's heat and enjoy a cool drink. It was once a home with a prosperous family and children.

When Shamus tore out walls and remodeled, there was one feature he could not uproot. He has learned she was a nanny around 1928. For some reason, the unhappy woman hanged herself in what is now the bathroom. Some patrons have seen her in a mirror near the back of the bar. Although she has never appeared to him, Shamus has still had encounters with her. "One night, I was here on my own and I was cleaning the place. I took all the ashtrays off the tables, put them on the bar to wipe the tables and then put them back. I must have missed some of the tables because when I came in next morning, all the ashtrays were sitting on the stools. I was the only one with keys so no one else could have come in and done it."

When he told some of his friends, they just didn't believe him. He said they told him, "'You're full of it!' I kept trying to tell them it had happened when suddenly that light"- he pointed to a spotlight aimed at "The Irish Republic"- "went off. Now that's a halogen light. When they blow, they blow. They don't come back on. That one did. It came back on. It wasn't the electricity or anything. Now those guys won't go in the bathroom unless three of them go in together."

Perhaps the nanny did not like her efforts to maintain a clean environment disparaged. As Shamus pointed out, "She looks after the place. She is a good spirit. Now every night when we leave, we salute her."

The spirit still harbors some jealousy towards other females. When there is live music, she never bothers the male musicians but often plays tricks on the female ones by playing with their sound system. Maybe it's a form of revenge. Perhaps in life, she lost her lover to another woman, driving her to suicide.

Those who are familiar with authors know we always like our books displayed to best advantage. We don't always agree with storeowners who have their own plans for displaying books. One St. Petersburg bookstore, Haslam's, is still dealing with a long dead author who changes the placement of his books.

Jack Kerouac, the renowned beatnik writer, spent the last years of his life in St. Petersburg. During that time, he frequently came into Haslam's and moved his books to higher locations, eye-level to patrons, to give them more prominence.

Haslam's owner, Charles Haslam, preferred to arrange books in alphabetical order. He would explain this to Kerouac to no avail. After Kerouac's death, the books began to mysteriously fly off shelves and move around of their own accord. Could it be the writer's spirit returning to Haslam's to rearrange the books as he had in life?

Area hotels also are inhabited by a bevy of permanent residents. Perhaps the best known of these spirits is found at the Don Cesar. This St. Petersburg landmark grew out of one man's ill-fated romance. Perhaps the dashing "Don Cesar" and his beautiful "Maritana" were doomed from the start. Then again, perhaps they have finally reunited in the afterlife and are now living their dream "life" for all eternity in their castle by the sea overlooking the azure waters of Tampa Bay. You decide for yourself.

He was an orphaned American raised by his Irish grandfather. He was sent to England for an education and there met a young opera singer named Lucinda. She was singing the female lead in Thomas Rowe's favorite opera, *Maratina*. The two fell madly in love and planned to elope and spend their lives in a pink castle by the sea.

It was not to be. Lucinda's parents intervened and, on the day they were to depart for the United States, kept Lucinda secreted away. The brokenhearted young Rowe had no choice. He had to return home as his guardian required but he never forgot his first love. He wrote to her at first but the letters came back unopened.

Throughout the ensuing years, Thomas became a wealthy man. Forced by ill health, he moved to Florida. It was there that he bought eighty acres of an island on the shores of Tampa destined to become St Petersburg Beach. He had since married another woman but his heart still yearned for the dream he had shared with his Lucinda. Now, a man of forty-two, he had the location and the means to build what he had promised his first love as a young student.

Finding Florida's Phantoms

He divided the acres of his island paradise into tracts and sold lots. The streets were named for characters and places in *Maritana*. But the crowning jewel in his kingdom by the sea was the ten-story Moorish Mediterranean pink hotel. It could only be called the "Don Cesar." In the sunroom on the ground floor, Rowe placed the fountain he had once promised to Lucinda. A winged angel poured water from a vase into a pond below encircled by swans.

The setting was gorgeous, the location was perfect but the timing was terrible. The Don opened on January 16, 1928 with a scene that would have fit a F. Scott Fitzgerald novel. However when the stock market crashed in October 1929, the reverberation were destined to shake even the ten-foot thick walls of Rowe's dream hotel.

Through receivership, hurricanes and prohibition, Rowe managed to hang on to his management of the hotel. Finally, he received a note from his lost love. Lucinda wrote on her deathbed to her beloved, "Time is infinite. I wait for you by our fountain . . . to share our timeless love, our destiny is time." Rowe died in the hotel on May 5, 1940. On his deathbed, he attempted to will the hotel to the staff. However, his doctors stated he was too ill to make a rational decision. His estranged wife, Mary, inherited it instead and took over the management. The hotel declined.

During the war years, the army purchased it. It became a hospital, a convalescent center, a veteran's administration office and finally a derelict almost ready for the demolition ball. During the time of government ownership, its angel fountain was removed and the floor tiled over. Why? Probably the same reason they painted it Government Issue Green.

Then in the 70's, it was rescued and on its way to being a world class hotel again. It was at this time that Thomas Rowe and his ladylove, Lucinda, began to be sighted by guests and staff alike.

The hotel passed through several hands and a few restorations but the two spirits still seem to be there. They have been joined by some from the era when the building was used as a hospital also.

People who worked with him reported smelling a foul smell like his cigarettes. Thomas had asthma and had to smoke certain cigarettes that the doctors prescribed that contained a medicine that got to his lungs. They had a particularly nasty smell.

Susan Owen, Director of Guest Services, recounted when the sightings began in earnest. "It was during the renovation. Workman would ask, 'Who was that white-haired man asking questions about the renovation?' Some of the workers refused to work here because of him. He never appeared as a wraith. It was always as a normal man."

There was one time he appeared to a journalist. It was not to give an interview but to help prevent tragedy. Susan struggled to recall the exact details but memory of the main incident was sharp. "She was a writer for, I think, Bride Magazine. They were doing an article about weddings here. The next morning she came down and asked. 'Do you have a ghost here?' The answer, of course, was 'yes, why.'

"The writer continued 'Last night in bed, a man appeared to me and said, 'Do not let her go on the ledge.' We asked what he looked like. The journalist made a sketch of the man and he bore a striking resemblance to Thomas Rowe.

Kathleen Walls

No one thought any more of it until a few days later when her photographer was doing a layout with the writer and a model on the rooftop. The rooftop there is actually a patio for the penthouse. The photographer wanted the model to get up on the ledge and get a shot of her. When he said 'ledge' bells went off in the writer's head. She stopped the shoot and when they examined the ledge found bits of crumbled mortar on top. Had the model stepped there she might have lost her balance and fallen."

Susan has had personal experiences with him. She has never seen him but she still finds little things happening that are unexplainable. "They only seem to happen to me when I am really rushing around doing something for a guest. For instance, the elevators are slow in the building. Usually I stand there and twiddle my thumbs while I count as the light tells the floors. 10, 9, 8 and so on. But if someone has forgotten something and I am rushing to get it back to him, inevitably, the elevator door opens just as I approach. No buttons pushed! No waiting! It is just there when I need it."

One receptionist who had come from Pennsylvania was temporally staying in the hotel. She and her husband were on the beach and she looked up and saw a man in a white linen suit and a Panama hat. She called to her husband, "Look, that looks like Panama Jack." Her husband didn't see the man. She just thought he must have disappeared behind the bushes and gave it no more thought until she was doing her orientation and spotted a picture of Thomas Rowe.

Thomas seems to be very protective of "his" hotel still. Once when a bride's mother was very upset and blaming the hotel for just about everything, she was raving at the florist in the hotel. Suddenly all the shelves in the refrigerators holding flower displays came crashing down. That not only silenced the lady but also sent her scuttling away.

Another place Thomas Rowe shows himself frequently is in the kitchen. Workers will suddenly see a face in one of the freezers and then it will be gone as fast as it appeared.

Many people have reported seeing a man and woman in period clothing walking around near where the original fountain was. Is it possible that Thomas and Lucinda do in fact "share our timeless love"?

Nurses and service men are also seen. Nurses in 1940's uniform are often carrying an armload of supplies. They are usually just walking and disappear into a wall.

A little way down the beach is a wondrous haven of peace and tranquility called Safety Harbor. Since pre-recorded history, this magic spot has been a Mecca for those seeking the healing powers of its springs.

Hernando de Soto in 1539 was the first European to sample the curative powers of the springs. He thought he had discovered what Ponce De Leon had missed, the Fountain of Youth. He named them Esperito Santo Springs (Springs of the Holy Spirit). The Native Americans had already known of the curative powers of the springs for thousands of years.

Through the late 1800's and early 1900's, a series of entrepreneurs tried to exploit the springs but it was not until 1945 that Dr. Salem Baranoff bought the sanatorium and springs and provided overnight accommodations for spa guests. Its guest list read like a Who's Who of the world's rich and famous, The Great Houdini, department store moguls F.W. Grant and Russ Kresgeand and their contemporaries came in droves.

Finding Florida's Phantoms

When you visit Safety Harbor, you find so much more than the spa that has made it famous. You find a quaint Florida town. Its Main Street boasts unique shops and art galleries. In its small city square, musicians perform beneath the Victorian style gazebo. You can find any type of food you want from the fast food with flair served at the little Whistle Stop café - try the fried green tomatoes there - to the health conscious yet delicious Spa food.

If are very observant you may find more that meets the eye there as well. Dining Room Manager, Tom Lamonica, decided to stay over at the spa one night because of an early morning schedule. He was cutting through the East Room to the kitchen to get some orange juice when suddenly all the lights came on. He called to the security guard that he believed had turned them on, "Chuck?" He then observed the Palm Lobby door opening slowly, all by itself. Chuck, the guard was at the front desk the entire time.

He had no choice but to attribute the occurrences to Dr. Baranoff. Tom reported other run-ins with the departed former owner. He is very particular about the table settings. Saltshakers are always set to the right of the pepper. No matter who sets the tables, Tom religiously checks these details. However, on many occasions, he had checked and found everything set to his satisfaction, then returned to the room a few minutes later to find the salt shakers switched with the pepper. Knowing that Dr. Baranoff did not allow salt on the premises, he feels, "Maybe he is trying to tell me something."

Other employees have had encounters of the strange kind. Night Manager John Vitucci went into the kitchen to turn off the lights, On his return trip, he almost fell over a large room service tray that wasn't there minutes before.

Perhaps the prize for the most bizarre incident goes to Administrative Assistant Stephany McHale. Stephany noticed that every time she went into the Signature Shop, a large bronze dog had been moved to a different location. One day as she passed a full three feet away from the dog, it suddenly lunged and struck her squarely on the knee. Stephany had the last laugh though. She banished the dog to the History Hall for biting an employee.

Lisa Wilkins was cleaning late one night in the huge tiled spa fitness center when the television in the Ladies Waiting Area came on full blast by itself. Lisa's comment, "I was outta there and back to the housekeeping office fast."

This is not the only experience Lisa had. She was cleaning in the men's shower at night and heard a shower come on. When she went to investigate, there was no shower on and none of them was even damp. This time Lisa had a witness. Another housekeeper was working with her and witnessed the entire episode.

The Baranoff Theater is one of the places most likely to experience strange phenomena. Many people have seen or heard "Dr. Baranoff" in it. One worker was stacking dishes to return to the kitchen when he heard a melody coming from the speakers. He glanced toward the sound booth to see who was playing around there. Instead of spotting a familiar co-worker, he saw an elderly, white haired gentleman with hat and glasses. He had seen enough photos of the Spa founder to recognize him and got out of there fast.

In fact, more of the employees have seen the spirit of Dr. Baranoff than haven't. Many of the housekeepers are afraid to work in the Spa's Harbor House, Springs or Palm Buildings.

It isn't only workers who have seen or heard Dr. Baranoff. Mrs. Beth Myers, an elderly guest, visited the Spa several years ago. She was awakened one night in room 319 in the Springs Building by a tap on the shoulder. She later swore it was an apparition of Dr. Baranoff's long dead niece. The phantom told her, "Everything will be alright."

It was not all right, however. Mrs. Myers died shortly after returning home. Did the gentle warning help her prepare for the inevitable? Who knows?

Perhaps Dr. Baranoff and his staff are still looking after their guests.

If the spirits at the Spa are not enough for you, try visiting the Safety Harbor Museum of Regional History. The museum traces the history of the area's Native Americans who also enjoyed visiting "The Place Where Healing Waters Flow." Maybe some of them are still dipping in the crystal pools seeking eternal life. Or have at least some of the area residents found their "Eternal Life"?

Of course, if you get tired of "ghost hunting," there is a lot of other attraction in the Tampa Bay area. Busch Gardens offers entertainment to please every age. They do have a ghost experience of sorts; a 4D interactive movie called *Haunted Lighthouse*.

Starship Dining Yacht, Captain Nemo's Pirate Cruses, Dauphin Cruises and countless deep sea fishing vessels are just waiting for the sailors in the family.

Sun and surf, shopping, sports, art, theater and just about anything you might desire can be found in the area.

In fact, some of the resorts in the Bay area are offering so much on site it is hard to find time to get off-site and explore the rest of the sun coast. Places like Saddlebrook Resort, located on 480 landscaped acres just outside Tampa, combine the charm of a lush "walking village" with all the amenities anyone could desire; super pool, golf courses, tennis courts, fitness center, spa, two world class restaurants, sports and pool bars are a vacation in themselves.

The thing to do is allow yourself time to enjoy all that the area offers. A lot of time!

Contacts:

Tampa Bay Convention and Visitors Bureau
400 N. Tampa St. Suite 2800
Tanpa, FL 33602
(800) 826-8358
kernest@visittampabay.com
www.visittampabay.com

Tampa Theater
711 Franklin Street
Tampa, FL 33602
P.O. Box 172188
Tampa, FL 33672-0188
(813) 274-8982
gargoyles@tampatheatre.org
www.tampatheater.org

Finding Florida's Phantoms

Fatima Café
Brandon Cuban sandwiches
cheap and good but small and crowded

Lake Worth Playhouse
www.lakeworthplayhouse.org/
(561) 586-6410

Tampa Center Place
619 Vonderburg Dr.
Brandon, FL 33511
(813) 685-8888

Berns (most well known and best restaurant) http://www.bernssteakhouse.com/bs_frame.htm

Colombia Restaurant (The best place for Cuban food in Ybor City) http://www.columbiarestaurant.com/

Red Mesa (for REAL Mexican food in St. Pete) http://www.wallscomealive.com/pages/redmesa.html

Antonio's Pasta Grille for Italian
Temple Terrace

The Green Iguana Bar & Grill
(kind of Mexican/Southwest/American)

Henry Plant Museum
http://www.plantmuseum.com/

Tampa Rico Cigar Co (Ybor Square), where tabaqueros demonstrate old-fashioned cigar making.
East 7th Ave.
The Ybor City State Museum
1818 E. 9th Ave.

Ybor City Brewing Company
2205 N. 20th St.
Ybor Square
1901 N. 13th St.

Ybor City Ghost Walk
Tours depart at 6 p.m. from Joffrey's Coffee Company
1616 E. 7th Ave. Thursday to Sunday.

Ft Myers

"There is only one Fort Myers, and ninety million people are going to out about it." Thomas Edison made this prediction in 1885 when he discovered the tiny Florida village on the banks of the bamboo-lined Caloosahatchee River. He was so smitten with the tropical paradise kissed by balmy gulf breezes that he built his winter home there.

The impressive McGregor Boulevard lined with its majestic palms was once the resting place of over 100 Calusa Indians. The remains were re-interred elsewhere when the road was built but perhaps they are still guarding their ancient burial area. That would account for reports of a Native American dressed in his ceremonial clothing that is occasionally spotted here.

Many of the visitors who swarm to Fort Myers do so to visit the home Edison and the adjourning home of his friend, Henry Ford. The homes of these giants of industry and science are fascinating for the glimpse into the personal life of the two men who changed our lifestyles more than any other inventors of the twentieth century did.

As you approach the Edison estate, the first thing you see is the gigantic Banyon Tree. Actually "gigantic" falls far short of describing this tree. His friend, Harvey Firestone, sent it to him from India. He wrote of the small sapling, "Plant this where it has plenty of room. I'm told it spreads." Spread it did! It now covers over 400 feet. Multiple trunks, limbs and roots intertwine to create a fantasy panorama.

The estate's 14 acres are covered with unusual trees and plants. Edison was a dedicated botanist. He collected unusual plant from all over. Small gardens, such as the one just outside his lab honoring his second wife Mina Edison, sprout all over the grounds.

Mrs. Edison was a great admirer of John James Audubon. She had an aviary installed on the grounds. In spring and summer, you can admire the bright plumage of the tropical birds. She also liked to swim, so Edison installed the first swimming

Finding Florida's Phantoms

pool in Florida in 1910. He provided cement from his own company in New Jersey and had it poured between forms. The pool still is in good condition today. Incidentally, Edison never swam in it. He didn't believe in exercise. In spite of this, he lived to be eighty-four.

The house was designed by Edison himself and reflects the relaxed pleasant lifestyle that he cultivated in Florida. A fish, caught by his son, is mounted on the porch. These fourteen-foot wide porches were built surrounding the house and double French doors were installed on all four sides to help cool the home. The furnishing is authentic to the period. There is even a light switch installed by Edison that still works. This isn't ghostly shenanigans, just better manufacturing practices than we have today.

If you're lucky, Mina Edison will arrive as you tour her home and regale you with some of her recollections. No, this is not the ghost of the departed Mina but you will feel as if Mina has returned to tell you about her home. The lady portraying Mrs. Edison is quite authentic. The official line is that there are no ghosts in the Edison home but the ambience does make you feel as if either Henry or one of his contemporaries is lurking about.

Thomas Edison and Henry Ford had a lot in common. They met in 1896 and became instant friends. When the house adjourning Edison's Florida home, one he had originally designed for a former friend, came on the market in 1916, Ford purchased it for a summer retreat for his family. The home displays much of the original furnishings. A highlight of his home is the three early model Fords. The cars are preserved in excellent condition.

The Edison laboratory highlights his prodigious amount of inventions. It reflects a man whose business was also his hobby. Edison did like to relax sometimes. One of his favorite pastimes was fishing. One story about him is that he would frequently fish without any bait. This allowed him to think uninterrupted. He gave several fishing tournaments. That tradition is still followed today. The Southwest Tarpon Tournament is held annually the first week in July and draws anglers from all over the world.

When you tour the attached museum, you finally realize the scope of the man. His inventions ranged from cement to phonographs, from latex to light bulbs. Here you also find the personality of the man. His office shows his love of books. His love of the outdoors is best reflected in his early version of a "camper." He has one of his cars set up with a traveling kitchen in back so that he and his family and friends could enjoy the outdoors in comfort. He would have loved one of today's modern RVs.

But Fort Myers and the adjacent area offer so much more. Of course, the beaches and sunny climate are still a big draw. In the day, you can laze in the sun but at night, adventure of a different kind awaits.

Beached Whale Bar is one good place to start a ghost hunt. Their spirit is different. One visitor started to share part of his hamburger with a little brown dog that sat near the bar and looked hungry. He was amazed when the pooch just disappeared into thin air. Although some think the tourist may have had one too many drinks, others believe the apparition was the pet dog of the bar's former owner, Mary Galloway, who died there in a mysterious fire in 1955.

Fort Myers also offers a ghost tour that skillfully blends history and legend.

Kathleen Walls

Babcock Wilderness Adventures is an in-your-face opportunity to glimpse the natural world of Southwest Florida. Located just north of Fort Myers in Punta Gorda, it offers a 90-minute tour of the 90,000-acre Crescent B Ranch. Although the ranch raises the conventional cattle and vegetables, they have a unique product. They are one of the few licensed alligator ranches in Florida. They also have a protected herd of American Bison on the ranch. Because the original owner, Edward Vose Babcock, was conservation minded long before it became stylish, much of the ranch is preserved in its natural state. Part of this is the 10,000-acre Telegraph Cypress Swamp. The ninety minute swamp buggy tour transverses this swamp and often brings you face to face with deer, raccoon, eagles, many varieties of wading birds and countless other wildlife. They are working with a breeding program and have several caged Florida Panthers. You will definitely see at least one alligator. Often visitors see more alligators than they would like.

Two visitors who preferred a few less 'gators were Lawrence Fishbourn and Sean Connery. Their brush with the reptile came about when they were filming *Just Cause* at the ranch. There was one scene where they were retrieving a gun from a culvert channeling a small stream. As the two actors reached into the culvert, a large alligator burst forth from it. It only took the ranch hands a few minutes to remove the reptile. It took quite a bit longer for the director to coax the two movie heroes back to the scene.

You may want to sample the 'gator dishes in their Gator Shack Restaurant. Be sure and see the museum, which is housed in part of the movie set of *Just Cause*.

The Babcock's donated 65,000 acres to the state in the 1940's. Today that adjourning tract is the Cecil B. Webb Wildlife Management Area. It's a great place to observe wildlife.

Another great spot to watch a unique mammal, the manatee, is at Manatee Park. This park offers a manatee-viewing platform along the Orange River where Florida Power and Light discharge water from their plant. The water draws the manatees. They love to frolic here, where it is several degrees warmer than the surrounding stream.

Another unique attraction is E.C.H.O., Educational Concerns for Hunger Organization. They are busy developing simple agricultural techniques and producing better seeds and plants to fight world hunger, particularly in third world countries. A tour of their test farm in North Fort Myers provides an opportunity to see plants not found anywhere else in this country. They experiment with plants such as the Moringa tree and the winged bean. The Moringa is known as "mother's best friend." Its leaves provide a calcium and vitamin rich baby food and supplement for nursing mothers; the young pods and roots can be eaten. The foliage can feed livestock. Because of its fast growth, the trees can be planted to provide a living fence to protect the family garden. The winged bean provides a "supermarket on a stalk." The leaves can be eaten like spinach, the pods like green beans and the blossoms are delicious raw or fried. The dried beans are a substitute for butter or oil.

Along with one of the largest tropical plant collections in Florida, their nursery has such oddities as the Lipstick Tree, which looks like tiny lipsticks blooming. If squeezed, the pod stains fingers a bright red. This used to be used to color

Finding Florida's Phantoms

margarine. Another oddity is a berry that causes other foods to change their taste. They also offer many unique gardening techniques that can be used in home gardens. You can buy unusual plants and seeds as well as books in the gift shop. Free tours of their demonstration farm are offered at 10 A.M. on Tuesday, Friday and Saturday.

Of course, this only scratches the surface of what the Fort Myers area has to see and do. There are four major museums, Fort Myers Historical Museum, Bailey-Matthews Shell Museum, Useppa Museum and the Imaginarium, an interactive science museum for children.

There are at least four wilderness preserve areas including the famous J.N. "Ding" Darling Refuge. Art galleries, theaters, parks and gardens abound. One other spot you want to visit is The Exciting New Shell Factory. This newly renovated complex contains restaurants, shopping, exhibits and boat rentals.

One definitely unique state park is the Koreshan State Historical Site. Its founder, Cyrus Read Teed, believed we live not on the surface of the earth but within. Born on a New York farm in 1839, Teed served in the Union Army and later set up a "medical" practice relying on herbal cures. When he developed his theory, he considered it not only a scientific revelation but also a religious one. He penned *The Cellular Cosmogony or, the Earth a Concave Sphere*, which he wrote under the pseudonym of Koresh, the Hebrew translation of "Cyrus."

Teed, who now called himself Koresh, offered a $10,000.00 reward to anyone who could confute his theory; no one did.

Teed abandoned his career and family and proclaimed himself the messiah of a new religion called Koreshanity. He established the World's College of Life in Chicago, and began publishing the Flaming Sword, a magazine. Strange as his theories were, he attracted followers and donations with which he bought a 300-acre tract in Florida in 1894 and founded a community called the Koreshan Unity, Inc.

He believed he would eventually have 10 million converts but only 250 actually settled there.

When Teed died in 1908, his followers, believing his statements that he would rise again, waited for this event in vain.

Teed's body was interred in an immense mausoleum with a twenty-four hour guard until his tomb was washed away by a hurricane in 1921. In 1961, his settlement was turned into the Koreshan State Historic Site, and Koresh's disciples offered guided tours until the last one died in 1982. It is believed some of his followers are still waiting for their leader to return to them even after their death. The site offers what they refer to as "Ghost Walks."

Captiva and Sanabel

You will want to visit nearby Captiva and Sanabel Islands. The Sanabel Lighthouse is one of the most frequently photographed spots in the area.

Boca Grande Lighthouse is said to be haunted by at several spirits. A former keeper, McKinnely, had a child who died in the dwelling. She can still sometimes be heard playing in a second floor entranceway. People have reported hearing the voice of a little girl and the sound of her playing jacks.

Kathleen Walls

At the turn of the century, one of the lighthouse assistants committed suicide in the assistant's house next to lighthouse. He is also believed to remain on the site.

The best known ghost of the Boca Grande Lighthouse is Jose Gaspar. Gaspar, or Gasparillo as he came to be known, was a well-born Spaniard. His love of adventure and women seems to have been his undoing. At age 12, he kidnapped a young local girl and held her for ransom. He was captured and the judge gave him the choice of entering the Royal Spanish Naval Academy or going to jail. He chose a life at sea. The navy was too tame for him; he became a pirate. His modus-operandi was to kill all the men and enounce the women in his harem. One particularly beautiful senorita, Josefa, the daughter of the Viceroy of Spain, enthralled him. Normally, the pirate kept all his captive women on Captiva (That is what it is named for.) He brought Josefa to Boca Grande instead. When she refused his advances, he cut off her head. A headless woman is reportedly seen walking the beach wearing a flowing dress but no head.

Pine Island is another of the islands off the coast where pirates buried treasures. Capt'n Con's Fish House in Bokeelia, is reputed to have many paranormal occurrences such as the dumpster lid slamming up and down, voices, and loss of breath. There have even been reports of sightings there as well as orbs captured on film. The restaurant at the northern tip of Pine Island has long attracted ghost hunters. The owner, Loretta Williams-Sims, admits she hasn't seen the alleged apparitions, but others have seen a spectral man and woman.

.A more recent spirit is said to wonder the area near Bonita Beach road and I-75. A homeless man called Cowboy was killed near there by a drinking buddy named Bubba on April 17, 1999. The two argued over some beer and Bubba hit Cowboy in the head with a concrete block and then stabbed him to death with a screwdriver. Bubba later confessed and is serving his sentence in prison. But residents of the area claim still to hear Cowboy playing the harmonica he always carried in life.

Cabbage Key

Perhaps on one of the best-loved islands off the Lee County Coast is Cabbage Key. Visitors to the island, which must be reached by boat, stay or dine at an inn that was originally built in the 1930's by Mary Roberts Rinehart.

The Inn dining room is decorated with a collection of over thirty thousand one dollar bills signed by patrons and stapled to the walls of its bar. It is built on top of a Calusa Indian shell mound.

It offers guestrooms or cottages for overnight visitors. The Inn's restaurant is famous for its "Cheeseburger in Paradise," believed to be the inspiration for the Jimmy Buffett tune.

In spite of its small size, the inn has one permanent guest. I do mean permanent. Both guests and employees alike have seen an apparition of a middle-aged woman with long brown hair dressed in thirties style clothing. She enters the bedrooms and strolls around, then leaves without bothering to open the door. She has also been known to throw things around in the kitchen. The staff believes she does not like changes made to the menu.

Finding Florida's Phantoms

She fits the description of a guest who came to visit the Rinehart's from New York. She came to stay with them in hope of recovering from her illness, tuberculosis. Unfortunately, she died there and is still trying to maintain things as they were when she lived.

Of course, the inn is built on a Calusa shell mound, as is much of the Lee County Coast; it is entirely possible that there may also be a Native American spirit there as well. And don't forget the pirates who buried much of their treasure up and down this coast. Is it not possible that their ghosts still roam the coastline seeking their bottle of rum?

Fort Myers and its surrounding area have not only lived up to Thomas Edison's prediction. It has far surpassed it.

Contacts:

Fort Myers Area Chambers
Sanibel-Captiva Islands Chamber of Commerce
1159 Causeway Rd., Sanibel, FL 33957
239-472-1080
www.sanibel-captiva.org

Boca Grande Chamber of Commerce
P.O. Box 704, Boca Grande, FL 33921
941-964-0568
www.bocagrandechamber.com

Bonita Springs Chamber of Commerce
25071 Chamber of Commerce Dr.
Bonita Springs, FL 34135
239-992-2943
www.bonitaspringschamber.com

Cape Coral Chamber of Commerce
P.O. Box 100747, Cape Coral, FL 33910
239-549-6900
www.capecoralchamber.com
Estero Chamber of Commerce
P.O. Box 588, Estero, FL 33928
239-948-7990
www.estero.org

Fort Myers Beach Chamber of Commerce
17200 San Carlos Blvd.
Fort Myers Beach, FL 33931
239-454-7500, (800) 782-9283
www.fmbchamber.com

Greater Fort Myers Chamber of Commerce
P.O. Box 9289, Fort Myers, FL 33902
239-332-3624
www.fortmyers.org

Greater Pine Island Chamber of Commerce
P.O. Box 525, Matlacha, FL 33909
239-283-0888
www.pineislandchamber.org

Lehigh Acres Chamber of Commerce
4109 Lee Blvd. A-nd Douglas Ave.
Lehigh Acres, FL 33971
239-369-3322
www.lehighacreschamber.org

North Fort Myers Chamber of Commerce
3323 N. Key Drive
Suite 6
North Fort Myers, FL 33903
239-997-9111

The Beached Whale
1249 Estero Blvd.
Fort Myers Beach Fl, 33931 463-5505

Ghost Tours
949-3644
www.hauntedfortmyers.com
jftwar@att.net

Cabbage Key, Inc.
P.O. Box 200
Pineland, FL 33945
Tel: (239) 283-2278
Fax: (239) 283-1384
http://www.cabbage-key.com/

Capt'n Con's Fish House Restaurant
8421 Main St. Bokeelia 33922
283-4300

Naples

From the wild life to the high life, Naples has it all. It sets on the doorstep of the Everglades. It's also the home of more millionaires than any other city its size in the country and a few spirits from bygone days as well..

Less than a century ago, Naples and all of Collier County were considered a worthless swamp. But during the gilded age when it was fashionable to winter in the Sunny South, advertising mogul Barron Collier began buying up southwest Florida land hand over fist. Lots of the land sat on top of ancient Calusa middens but he never considered that he was getting something more than he bargained for, ghosts. He foresaw visitors trekking south to enjoy the pristine beauty and balmy gulf breezes. How right he was! Still, he never considered the beings that were already there and not going anywhere.

A great way to get an overview of Naples is to hop aboard the Trolley Tour. Your guide will cover at least 100 points of interest and you can disembark and re-board all over the city. You will see the obvious points of interest, such as Palm Cottage, one of Florida's last "tabby houses" dating back to 1895. But you'll also find out a lot of whimsical facts. For example, as you pass an Eckerds Drugs, your driver will point out a wrought iron fence with headstones inside. "Rose Mary Cemetery," he comments. "What's a cemetery doing in the middle of a parking lot? Well, it was moved there in 1937 to accommodate expansion. It was deeded so that whoever bought the land would have to build around it so that it would never have to be moved again. That was all rural land those days. No one lived for miles around. So that's why you find a cemetery in the middle of an Eckerds' parking lot."

Palm Cottage is the second oldest home in Naples. Built in 1895, Palm Cottage is listed on the National Register of Historic Places but it should be on a list of National Register of Haunted Places, too. Alexandra Brown, who died in 1978, still roams around Palm Cottage slamming doors, mostly on the second floor. Locals have even seen her wave to them from a second floor window.

On Sunday before she died, she had laid out her husband's uniform on their bed and placed a black rose on her pillow. Did she know of her impending death?

There also seems to be another spirit there, the little boy who died in a fire next door. So it is well worth looking deeper than just the trolley tour pass by.

Old Naples General Store is the logical place to embark on your trolley journey. You can purchase your tickets there as well as stock up on some delicious candy, buy souvenirs, pick up tourist information and experience the way people shopped in Naples at the turn of the century. They also have a large parking lot that will easily accommodate an RV.

Tin City is one place you definitely want to stop and explore. Tin City began life as an oyster and clam processing plant in the 1920's. In 1976, it began its reincarnation as the Old Marine Market Place. Today, Tin City combines the ambience of the city's nautical past with unique shops and eateries. This is also the boarding dock of many of the sightseeing and fishing boats.

Although Naples is filled with sunshine, the Double Sunshine is a special treat. It transports you over the magical waters of Naples Bay. Here you observe the homes of the rich and famous in Port Royal as dolphins frolic around your boat. The more you applaud the dolphins' antics, the more they cavort. You can practically touch them from the lower deck of the boat.

If you enjoy fishing, the Lady Brett or Captain Paul departs from the same dock. The Captain Paul also has a shelling trip. They transport you to Keewaydin Island Beach where you can search for Sand Dollars, Conchs and a host of other iridescent beauties. If you want a charter boat, Fish Finder Charters is the place. It's also the home of the one and only Bubbles Vanderbilt, a well-dressed potbellied pig who actually has her own web site. Fishing and water fun has always been a big part of Naples. The Silver Slam Tarpon tournament and the Great Dock Canoe Races reflect Naples love affair with the sea.

If you yearn to take a walk on the wild side, visit Caribbean Gardens. Like any life story, the garden's saga is one of ups and downs. It was begun in 1919 by Dr. Henry Nehrling as Tropical Gardens, one of Florida's earliest arboretums. It gained a worldwide reputation during his lifetime but degenerated with his death in 1929.

More than twenty years passed and the once lush garden became an overgrown jungle. Then Julius Fleischmann, of the yeast and Standard Brands family, discovered the gardens and began a loving restoration. He cleared away years of neglect and brought Dr. Nehrling's dream to life once more. He added a dazzling array of tropical birds and, in 1954, reopened the gardens under its present name, Caribbean Gardens.

The next step in the garden's metamorphism came in 1967 when "Jungle" Larry Tetziaff and his wife, Nancy Jane, fell in love with the serene setting and attempted to acquire it for their animal exhibit. They had both spent their lives working with wild life and carrying a message of conservation to the world, mainly through a combination of rarely seen filmed footage of the habitat and activities in the wild combined with the living animals. They were then sharing their love of nature with over a million visitors a year at their Ohio location. Naples climate was what they wanted for their jungle friends. However, it wasn't until shortly after Fleischmann's death that their dream of combining the beauty of the tropical flora with their exotic fauna became a reality. In September 1969,

Finding Florida's Phantoms

the gardens threw open its gates to an unprecedented offering of many of the earth's rarest creatures in a setting of some of the world's most beautiful plants.

The best place to start your tour is at Safari Canyon where you will be treated to a multimedia show unlike any you have seen. You learn about the animals in their natural environment on huge screens, then meet the actual creature up close and personal. Speaking of "meet," the Meet the Keeper Series is a great place to ask all those questions about your favorite animal to the person who knows it best, the keeper.

The variety of big cats is unsurpassed. Be sure to see the rare White Tigers and the even rarer Honey Colored Tigers. If you have children with you, you may want to get a "ZOOKEY" which provides valuable information via an audio station at each site.

Primate Expedition Cruise is another favorite. You visit monkeys and other primates from around the world in a natural type habitat as you cruise in comfort around their islands.

For a closer look at the local wild life, try The Conservancy of Southwest Florida. The Conservancy has spearheaded the effort to maintain nature's delicate balance in a rapidly progressing society since 1964 when they stopped the building of a highway through the environmentally delicate Rookery Bay. A visit to the Naples Nature Center is the best value for your vacation dollar. (For $6 adults and $3 children, you tour both Naples and Briggs Nature Centers.) At the Naples center, book your electric boat tour and/or naturalist guided hike first. If you only have time for one, opt for the boat tour.

Then start with the Museum. There is always something going on there. You might find Snakes Alive, a program that will tell you all you ever wanted to know about serpents. Or perhaps its time for Simply Shells;, these iridescent jewels of the beach are not simple. Turtle Talk, featuring the new turtle exhibit, or a guided trail walk are also programs you will enjoy.

Their rehabilitation center provides the most advanced care to the injured wildlife brought there daily. You can peep in on the treatment center through the special closed circuit television. Visit with an American eagle, owl, pelican and hawk that live there permanently. Because of their injuries, they cannot be returned to the wild.

When it's time for your boat tour, one of the volunteers like Capt. Jim Kussic will guide you through an estuary of the Gorden River. You are surrounded by Red Mangroves, Brazilian Pepper Trees and Australian Pine. He recounts the lore of the Calusa Indians, the history of the area, gossip about the residents past and present and as much scientific information about the native flora and fauna as you want to know. You will probably see herons, turtles and other wildlife.

If you are in the mood for hiking, the trails wend their way through 14 miles of woodland.

Briggs Center, located on Rookery Bay, boasts a butterfly garden, an interpretive center, two nature trails and a half mile of board walk from which you are sure to spot many of the wading birds, herons, egrets, anhingas and many other species that use the area for a hatchery. Both centers offer canoe and kayak rentals.

Kathleen Walls

For more nature adventures, Naples is located just a few miles from the Big Cypress Swamp; Corkscrew Swamp Sanctuary and Fakahatchee Strand Preserve are nearby and offer glimpses of the Everglades ecosystem. Two state parks are also close by. Wiggens Pass State Park offers day adventures and an excellent sandy beach for swimming and shelling. Collier Seminole offers camping as well as boat rentals and picnic facilities.

Collier County Museum is a great place to delve into the history of Naples and Collier County. If you plan to visit the first weekend in November, be sure to attend their Old Florida Festival. This is held annually on the museum grounds and celebrates 6,000 years of South Florida history. The booths are arranged as camps from the First Floridians to World War ll. The pride of the museum is their newest exhibit, an authentic World War ll Sherman Tank.

Of course, the festival also features entertainment, food and arts and crafts.

Art of all kind is well represented in Naples. Several art and music events are held throughout the year including Art in the Park and Naples Concert Band. Both run from January to April. The Naples Downtown Art Festival is held annually in March.

One place to stay for the ghost conscious visitor is the Olde Marks Island Inn. The inn, like so much in that area, was built on an old Calusa Indian mound. This might account for some of the strange happenings here. Sailors from the time of Ponce de Leon stopped here to refill their casks with the cool artesian water. But it wasn't until Captain Bill Collier built his inn here in 1883 that the spot became a traveler's landmark. Today it is a registered historic landmark.

The original inn had 20 sleeping rooms, and a two-story outhouse. The outhouse was the only one of its kind and was featured in Ripley's "Believe it or Not" column. Collier's building is one of the oldest in the area.

Calusa artifacts have been discovered here with the most famous being the Marco Cat found just a few yards from where the Inn stands. In 1999, the inn was restored by owner/decorator Marcy Kruchten and expanded.

The Inn has one other thing, a ghost that inhabits the original building, now the lobby & dinning room. Possibly one of the Calusa or an early guest that met an unfortunate end. It has been heard at night walking up the stairs, then opening and closing a door. It is also reported to move things like chairs around the premises.

Naples is a city of glitter and glitz but it's just a friendly small town at heart. It lives up to its slogan "Florida's Most Gracious City." Wonder if they ever considered "Florida's Most GhostlyCity?"

Contacts:

Naples General Information
www.see-naples.com

Naples Trolley Tours
(941) 262-7300

Finding Florida's Phantoms

Lady Brett, Capt. Paul, Double Sunshine
(904)263-4949
Collier County Museum
(94) 774-8476
www.colliermuseum.com

Caribbean Gardens
1590 Goodlette-Frank Rd
Naples Florida 34102
ZooLine (239) 262-5409
www.caribbeangardens.com

Tin City
941-262-4200
www.tin-city.com

Conservancy
(941) 262-CARE
www.conservancy.org

Bubbles Vanderbilt
www.bubbles-vanderbilt.com_

Olde Marco Island Inn and Suites
100 Palm Street
Marco Island, Florida 34145
(877) 475-3466
mail@oldmarco.com

Top: The Don Cesar in St. Petersburg
Bottom: Edwardo Martinez Ybor and his wife's urn at Merle Kelce Library
Photos by Kathleen Walls

Finding Florida's Phantoms

Top: Shamus Hannigan at the James Joyce Pub in Ybor City
Bottom: Henry Plant's former hotel, now The University of Tampa
Photos by Kathleen Walls

Top: Sanabel Lighthouse
Bottom: Cabbage Key Inn is papered with money
Photos by Kathleen Walls

Southeast
Homestead

When fickle sixteen-year-old Agnes Scuffs jilted her fiancée on the eve of their wedding, she set in motion a series of events that would lead to the construction of a monument comparable to Stonehenge. She informed Ed Leedskalnin that he was too old and too poor for her. Broken hearted, Ed left his native Latvia and settled near Florida City. He began carving a memorial to his lost love who he always referred to as "Sweet Sixteen."

Thus, The Coral Castle could also be called Love's Labor Lost. Fortunately for us, it's not lost. It's located in Homestead. These gigantic coral rock formations, some weighing as much as 29 tons, were created by Ed who stood five foot tall and weighed 100 pounds. What makes these sculptures even more miraculous is that Ed Leedskalnine used no power tools, just simple block and tackles, winches and wedges, many of them homemade from junkyard parts. He worked alone, usually at night, and told no one his secret for moving the giant rocks.

Over twenty years, he created a castle and all its furnishings out of the solid rock he quarried. He dedicated the entire estate to "Sweet Sixteen," often referring to her as if she were due to arrive any day.

The walls of the castle are made of giant stone with the cracks between filled so perfectly by smaller ones that you cannot see light between them. He fashioned a bedroom with beds for himself and "Sweet Sixteen" as well as children's furniture for his hoped for children. Many men put their loves on a pedestal. Ed fashioned a throne for her as well as for himself. He also made one for his future mother-in-law. This he made the most uncomfortable in the castle. Perhaps Ed had something of the realist in him after all.

His romanticism shows most in the Feast of Love Table. It is heart shaped and weighs 5,000 pounds. However, his crowning achievement is the Nine-Ton Gate. Despite its weight, the gate can be turned by a child with one hand and fits within a quarter of an inch of its surrounding walls.

During his lifetime, visitors marveled at his workmanship but he never revealed how he did it. Some have surmised Ed knew the secrets of the pyramids. Many of his carvings do show an interest in astronomy. The Polaris Telescope, which he created out of almost thirty tons of rock, focuses perfectly on the North Star. His Sun Dial is so accurate you can determine the time within one or two minutes. The Crescent Moon and Planets, the moon alone weighs 23 tons, The Moon Fountain, containing three phases of the moon, and the Great Obelisk, larger than the great upright at Stonehenge, all indicate knowledge of the heavenly bodies.

For a man so obsessed, Ed had a sense of humor as evidenced by the Florida Table. It is a twenty-foot long table shaped like the Sunshine State and surrounded by ten stone chairs. Ed envisioned the governor at the head chair and senators and representatives at the others, discussing ways to raise taxes.

After his death, people have reported mysterious happenings at the site. Photographs taken show "people" that were not present in the actual photograph. One psychic has claimed to contact Ed but no one has yet discovered his secret.

The only person with whom Ed would have gladly shared his knowledge was not interested. Although she knew of the Coral Castle for many years, "Sweet Sixteen" never visited it. When Ed died of stomach cancer in 1951, he took the secret to his grave.

Whatever you choose to believe about Ed and his castle, you have to accept that although he had only a fourth-grade education, Ed was an outstanding engineer. When Hurricane Andrew devastated much of the surrounding area in 1992, the castle wasn't affected at all.

Once when the huge back gate became stuck in open position, it took a crew of six workers almost two days to correct the problem and reseat the gate using a mechanized winch and crane. Ed was able to do it half a century ago with only hand tools and his own puny manpower.

In 1984, the Coral Castle was placed on the National Register of Historic Places. It alone makes Homestead, Florida worth a visit. But there are lots of other reasons to visit this South Florida area.

Of course, the white sand beaches and sparkling ocean waves are a big attraction, but there is a lot more.

Homestead and Florida City are a treat for eyes weary of snow and ice. The entire area is abloom throughout the year. Even when the rest of the country is locked in winter's fiercest grip, **bright red tomatoes**, vivid yellow squash, orange trees drooping under their succulent burden, all these and more burst from the earth.

Homestead welcomes its yearly influx of visitors with a renovated historic area. (Much of this area was devastated by Hurricane Andrew in 1992.) The center of the district is Old Town Hall, originally built in 1917. It hosts the Chamber of Commerce upstairs, recommended first stop for visitors, and a museum downstairs. In front, the street is cleverly worked in a brick mural. Across the street, the park, with its outdoor stage and flanking muraled wall, is ground zero for the Friday Fests. This is held on the first Friday of the month and offers

Finding Florida's Phantoms

musical entertainment and Classic Auto Shows. Another attraction you don't want to miss is the Fruit and Spice Park. You can eat far more than your admission cost in fallen tropical fruit. It's the largest collection of exotic plants and fruit in the country.

For dining and entertainment, the Main Street Cafe is a winner. They offer a varied menu including many vegetarian meals and feature soup, your choice of one of five, and unlimited salad. On weekend evenings, they have entertainment. Next door, you can surf the internet for $5 per hour.

Other events you can enjoy are the annual Rodeo, held in January, the Kiwanis Dolphin Tournament, Spritzer Dodge Great Sunrise Balloon Race and the Cinco de May Mexican Festival.

The city hall at Florida City is overrun with animals. Topiary animals, that is. The pieces add a whimsical touch. This is the gateway to Everglades National Park. Just before you enter the park there is one fruit stand you need to visit, Robert is Here.

Robert is Here is specializes in tropical fruit. You can browse stands full of unusual produce fresh from the fields. Added pieces of whimsy here are the animals in residence. There is the cat, usually found sleeping under the stands, the colorful talking Macaw, sitting on a ring in the store, and out back a collection of turtles and iguanas. If it's a hot day, try one of Roberts's tropical fruit smoothies.

These are some of the reasons many people return to the area each year. If you haven't been to Homestead/Florida City yet, you don't know what you are missing.

Contacts:

Coral Castle
(305) 248-6344

Everglades

Perched on the southern tip of the Florida peninsular is a land of watery beauty. This tropical Eden was once inaccessible to all but the hardiest travelers. Today, we can drive into this giant "river of grass" and enjoy its beauty in comparative luxury. We can sit in our motor homes and watch the sun's golden orb descend into the pewter waters of Florida Bay. We can stand by our barbecue pit and watch great flocks of white winged water birds swirl overhead. However, to come to know this vast ecosystem, we must leave the pavement behind and step into the real Everglades.

Sure, we might get our feet wet and muddy. We might experience a few mosquito bites. However, the reward of watching one of the few remaining American Crocodiles bask in the sun or experiencing the thrill of meeting a deer face to face makes it worthwhile. Who knows, we might even spot an elusive Florida Panther deep in a hardwood hammock. But we might find more than we bargain for. This is a place of mystery and ancient secrets. Things happen there that could not happen elsewhere.

One of the strangest occurrences in modern aviation began there at what should have been an ending.

It was the night of Friday, December 29th, 1972. Eastern Airlines Flight 401 with 176 people aboard neared its destination, the Miami Airport. The two men in charge of the landing were Captain Bob Loft and Second Officer Don Repo. The plane developed a problem and minutes later slammed into the Everglades. Final count left 103 people dead. Among them were Loft and Repo. A tragic story in itself but that isn't all there was to the story.

Eastern was able to salvage some parts of the aircraft. These were routinely put into other planes. And that's when the stories began drifting in. People, particularly crew members on those flights, began seeing strange things. Officer Repo would visit the cockpit and galleys. He seemed concerned with plane safety. He fixed a faulty oven circuit once in a galley. Another time, he pointed out a potential fire hazard and a hydraulic leak on a plane.

Finding Florida's Phantoms

Captain Loft was also seen. He usually was in a passenger's seat or the crew's cabin. One flight attendant questioned him since she could not identify him from the passenger list. When she called in the Captain to confront him, Loft just disappeared in front of her, the captain and a dozen passengers.

Even a vice president of Eastern Airlines apparently spoke to a phantom Loft once, believing him to be the captain in charge of the flight, before recognizing him as the dead captain.

Of course, Eastern disassociated itself and claimed the incidents never happened. They went so far as to threaten dismissal for anyone making any comments regarding any appearances of the two deceased officers. They threatened to sue the author of a book on the subject, John G. Fuller, who wrote *The Ghost of Flight 401,* as well as the producers of a television movie made from the book.

However, they did quietly order the removal of any of the 401's salvaged parts from other aircraft. When we think of The Everglades, most of us think of the National Park located there. However, the park comprises only about one fifth of The Everglades. It's designed to help protect at least a part of it.

Flamingo Campground is the most popular of the campgrounds, probably because it's the southernmost campground in the continental United States. Located on Florida Bay, it has 234 drive-in sites as well as walk-in and group sites, rest rooms, 2 dump stations, a restaurant, a post office, laundry facilities, a general store, marina, a visitor center/museum, public telephones and cold showers.

At the Flamingo Dining Room, you can let someone else do the work while you enjoy a view of the azure waters of Florida Bay.

The waterways have always been the biggest attraction here. You can enjoy anything from a short canoe or kayak trip to fully equipped houseboat rentals. The bay or backcountry cruises are great ways to explore the waterways. On the backcountry cruises, you may spot a sunning crocodile. There are only a few hundred of these endangered reptiles left. The southern tip of Florida is the only place in the U. S. they can be found. Be on the lookout for many varieties of birds, hawks, herons, terns and dozens of others. An alligator sighting is almost a given. These once endangered creatures abound.

The bay cruises, either the sunset sailing cruise or the four-hour Dolphin Cruise, are a place to spot dolphins, pelicans, ibis, egrets and numerous other birds. The dolphins are natural hams. They love to perform and the more you clap and cheer, the more they will entertain you. Just below the surface, you often spot Manatees drifting in the clear water.

The marina offers docking for your own boat and fuel, as well as rentals from canoes to fully furnished houseboats.

You can reserve a site November through April by calling 800-365-CAMP. Camping is limited to 14 days in the park during winter and 30 days per year. Current prices are $14 per day in winter, free from June to August. (If you come in the summer, bring a saddle. The mosquitoes are large enough to ride and very hungry.)

Take advantage of the numerous ranger led activities. For the braver of you, a sunset canoe trip or Slough Slog brings the swamp to life in a new way. There are dozens of ranger led programs for kids or grown-ups. For information on current activities, check at one of the visitor centers: Ernest F. Coe at the entrance, Flamingo Visitor Center at that campground and Royal Palm Visitor Center, midway between the entrance and Long Pine Key.

For bird watching or just getting away from it all, the many hiking trails, boardwalks or ponds are a perfect place to stretch out those highway kinks. Eco Pond, near Flamingo, sports flocks of wading birds nesting in the trees like so many giant cotton balls.

Paurotis Pond is a rookery area for Wood Storks and a possible place to spot Roseate Spoonbills. Mrazek Pond and Nine-Mile Pond also are good places for birding. If you really want to see one of the rare Flamingos, try Snake Bight Trail.

For nature at its best, Anhinga, Gumbo Limbo and Mahogany Hammock Trails offer you a chance to observe plant and animal life.

The "Don't Miss" spot is Shark Valley. Your $10 admission ticket to the park will get you into here also. If you only visit Shark Valley, off Highway 41 on the north end of the park, it will cost you $8 admission. You can take a wildlife-viewing tram, rent a bike, or just walk. Shark Valley is the best locale in the park for photographing wildlife. I once observed people clustered around a 14-foot alligator sunning on the pavement there. Suddenly he stirred. You won't believe how fast people can move. Incidentally, you are not allowed closer than 25 feet and feeding wildlife in the park carries a stiff fine. Be especially careful with small children and dogs. Children are closer to the size alligators recognize as prey and dogs fit in the hors-d-oeuvre category.

One elusive, some say mythical, creature that has been reported more than once is the Skunk Ape. Believers claim the creature is about seven feet tall, walks upright like a man, is covered with hair and has an awful smell.

The Gulf Coast Park Area in Everglades City is the jumping off point for a canoe trip through the Ten Thousand Islands, that no man's land of half-water-half-land, where the ocean mates with the gulf.

Big Cypress Swamp, named for its size rather than the diameter of the trees, provides more primitive camping.

The waterways along all the roadsides are a bubbling cauldron of wildlife. Plumed herons, rare Wood Storks and curved beaked ibises all prance and fish almost on top of giant sun soothed alligators. Beneath the clear surface of the water, needle nosed gar dart. On the trees, the bromeliads bloom, their scarlet flowers contrasting sharply with the tree trunks that support them.

The Loop Road by day is a haven for all kinds of birds, deer and the ever-present alligators. At night, it is a mysterious world populated with strange noises and rustling palmetto fronds. Park on a bridge here at night and point your flashlight over the water. The eerie red glow of ever-cruising eyes tells you the daydreaming alligators of several hours ago were merely recharging their solar batteries for night. Now, those sleepy reptiles are deadly killing machines.

If you're feeling adventurous, a 17-mile trip down washboard style Turner River Road will bring you under I-75 to Bear Island. According to Ranger Jeff Stead, this is the area you are most likely to find one of the elusive Florida Panthers. They are most active after dark. New breeding practices introducing the western panther, which is close enough genetically to interbreed, is creating a slight upswing in the population.

When you begin to feel like Crocodile Dundee and need a bit of civilization to balance your emotional checkbook, visit Everglades City just three miles from Big Cypress. It provides a small supermarket, a Laundromat and a public library where you can use the computer to check your e-mail. Suzie's Station features short order meals amongst memorabilia of bygone automotive history. They even sell packets of "Skunk Ape Food."

The Smallwood Store Museum, on Chokoloskee Island is a trip back to the Everglades at the turn of the century. Ted Smallwood opened the store to trade with the Seminoles. It was open until 1982 and on the National Registry of Historic Places since 1974. Today, Ted's granddaughter operates it as a museum.

However, if you listen closely you may hear ghostly screams. This was the place where one of the most horrible tragedies in the annals of migrant labor ended. Then again, maybe it didn't end with Ed Watson's death. Maybe what he did will cause haunting echoes here forever.

It was in 1910 that the first body was found, a woman a named Hanna Smith. A small-frightened runaway boy heralded the finding. He showed up at the store one day and would not, or could not, tell where he came from or why.

Investigations led to the Watson farm, a 40-acre shell-mound island, 17 miles south of Chokoloskee on the Chatham River. He was known as a man with a bad reputation already. He was a blue-eyed red haired Scotsman with a very bad temper. Rumors were that he had fled his family farm in Central Florida after killing a man there. Next, he was reputed to have become involved with the Belle Stare gang and believed to be the man who shot and killed the famous woman outlaw. There were stories that he had slit a man's throat in the Keys and killed at least four others before settling in the big swamp.

He raised winter vegetables to sell to the northern market and sugar cane to make syrup. Mostly folks left him alone. And that was fine with him. He liked his privacy.

Like many people in the area, Ed Watson hired migrant workers to help in his harvest. But when the job was finished, instead of paying them off and sending them home, he did the unthinkable. Watson killed his workers. To dispose of the evidence, he hacked up the bodies and fed them to alligators. He forced the boy to help him. When his atrocities became known, he tried to escape but a horrified posse awaited him. He was shot on the dock leading to the store when he tried to escape. The local people were in such dread of Watson that they buried his body 8 miles away at Rabbit Key.

Many a local will tell you he has heard sounds coming from the old swamp that are not animal and cannot be human. Screams heard like a woman in agony. Maybe like a woman being hacked to pieces before her young son's eyes. Swamp lights and other unexplained happenings still persist in the area.

The house Watson lived in was abandoned when his family left the area. A desperate woman with no place else to go tried to inhabit it once. She told of strange lights around the house and trees that seemed alive and advance on the house in the night. She soon left. The house fell into ruins and was reclaimed by the swamp. There is a primitive campground there called The Watson Place Campsite. If you want to, you can boat out there and camp overnight. Perhaps a silent Seminole poles his boat near the ruins occasionally and feels the presence still there. You do not want to visit this spot.

The Everglades was home to the Seminole and the Miccosukee people when the white man considered it only a useless wasteland. Both tribes have reservations here. You can visit their casinos, ride their airboats, eat in their restaurants (try the Fry Bread), tour their museums and, most importantly, learn from them.

Although he was a Plains Indian, Chief Seattle could have been speaking of the Everglades when he wrote these words. "There is no quiet place in the white man's city. No place to hear the unfurling of the leaves in spring or the rustle of insects wings. And what is there to life if one cannot hear the lonely cry of the whippoorwill or the argument of the frogs around a pond at night."

The Everglades is one of the few such places left on our planet where Chief Seattle would still feel at home.

Contacts:

Everglades National Park
40001 State Road 9336
Homestead, FL 33034-6733
(305) 242-7700 EVER_Information@nps.gov
www.nps.gov/ever/

Historic Smallwood Store
Post Office Box 367
Chokoloskee, Florida 33925
(239) 695-2989
Fax (239) 695-4454
www.florida-everglades.com/chokol/smallw.htm

Finding Florida's Phantoms

Top: Ed's astrological symbols have been interpreted to mean he knew the secrets behind building the pyramids
Bottom: The massive stone gate at Coral Castle weighs tons yet can be turned with just one finger
Photos by Martin Walls

**Keys
Key West**

Ever get an urge to check out some foreign exotic haunt? Well you can do that without ever leaving the U. S. Sort of. There are some that will argue that Key West isn't exactly part of the country. It declared its independence and named itself the Conch Republic.

The history of how that came to be is typical Key West. Key West, being the easternmost part of the United States and an island to boot, is a perfect haven for drug smugglers. Back in the 1980's, as part of a not too well thought out part of the government's War on Drugs, the DEA set up roadblocks on the Overseas Highway, the only road in and out of Key West. Well, the drug runners probably had the resources to either fly or boat their illegal cargo into the mainland but the tired commuters who work off island found themselves sitting in stopped traffic waiting hours to get home in the evenings.

Instead of taking things to court and proceeding the legal but slow way, they devised a simpler solution. They declared their independence from the United States, set up the Conch Republic and launched an attack on the federal military base there. No one got hurt in the ensuing battle as the Conchs, as they called themselves, used stale bread as their weapon of choice. After throwing the last of their floury ammunition at the Feds, they adjourned to Sloppy Joe's or one of the many other outdoor bars to celebrate their newfound independence.

Needless to say, the blockades were lifted and Key West was welcomed back into the fold with open arms. After all, where else would harried tourists go, if not the Key West, to unwind? Politics is not an important consideration; their idea of "party affiliation" means which bar do you prefer? Passports to their new country are still sold in all the gift shops. The main part of the Constitution they believe in is the part about "pursuit of happiness." In pursuit of this, they have more bars, restaurants and fun attractions than you would believe possible to cram into their tiny four mile wide island.

Of course the first stop is the shrine to fun favored by Papa Hemmingway, Sloppy Joe's. The original owner was Joe Russell and Hemmingway commented, "Joe you run a sloppy place, you should call this place Sloppy Joe's." Actually, it

Finding Florida's Phantoms

was across the street and down a ways but when they tried to raise Joe's $3 rent, he moved across the street. It is said they never shut the bar down; they just had the patrons pick up their drinks and move across the street with them.

The original site was the location of the present day Captain Tony's Saloon. Captain Tony's just has to have a ghost. For one thing, it was built on top of a morgue. When a hurricane blew down the morgue, several bodies must have been buried in the rubble. When they excavated to build the present building, several bodies were found. Since there was no money to relocate them, they were blessed and a concrete slab poured over them. Playing pool on top of some dead bodies gives a whole new aspect to the game.

If that wasn't enough to guarantee a haunting, the original tree used for hangings was located right outside the morgue for convenience. The most well know "hangee" is believed to be still hanging around the bar. She is called the Lady in Blue. Many years ago when Captain Tony lived above the bar, he saw a lovely young woman dressed in a long blue dress inside his courtyard. The gate was locked and there was no way she could have gotten in. Shortly after that when he was considering cutting down the large oak in the middle of the courtyard to expand, an old timer told him a story of one particular hanging on that tree.

A woman murdered her husband and children but her neighbor saw her and reported the crime. The woman was subsequently hanged from that tree. She chose to wear a long blue dress. Needless to say, Captain Tony left the tree and built around it. Patrons still occasionally report seeing a lady in a blue dress in the courtyard.

If you were expecting a ghost in The Hard Rock Café, you would expect to see Elvis or Buddy Holley. It's a shrine to rock and roll legends but the ghost there is from another era altogether.

It was built by William Curry, Florida's first millionaire, as a present for his son Robert. Robert was always a sickly soul. So when his father built the home for him and his bride, he spared no expenses. The elaborate gingerbread and the beautiful woodwork on the Victorian mansion testify to that. Although wealth could not protect Robert from his illness and the depression that accompanied it, the gradual loss of the family fortune drove him to commit suicide in a second floor bathroom.

The house was sold first to the Society of Elks who found they could not evict the original owner who continued to make his presence felt. They eventually gave up and the building passed through a multitude of hands until it became the Hard Rock Café. Robert is still there. He can be felt in the cold spot in the second floor rest room, in the opening and closing of file cabinets and moving items. People have even seen Robert in an upstairs window. So if you are enjoying a tasty treat in the old mansion and someone slips a taste of your food, maybe it isn't you dinner companion after all.

Of course, there is no shortage of eating and drinking spots in Key West. Margaretteville is a staple if you are a Jimmy Buffet fan. For something out the ordinary, try B.O. Fish House. You will enjoy first class seafood in a semi-outdoor setting. You can get acquainted with the cat while you eat but the owner asks you not to share your food with him. "Onions aren't good for Blackie."

Then there is the one and only Schooner Wharf Bar and Restaurant. It's one of the few places man's best friend is welcome to belly up to the bar. You might find yourself sitting next to a purebred poodle or a Conch mutt but they are all surprisingly well behaved. The bar's owner, Evelina Worthington, will be happy to show you the portrait of the Key West dogs hanging over the bar and tell you their story. It's located on the wharf right next to where the Key West Flag Ship, The Western Union, is docked.

The island's brawling and boisterous history provide opportunities for some pretty interesting ghosts. Even the original name of the place, Cayo Hueso, means "Bone Island." It was the hangout of pirates and wreckers. The wreckers would wait for a ship to go aground in a storm, then rush out to grab the booty. Although some considered the wreckers little better than pirates, they were honest hard working men plying a respectable trade. The best place to learn of the wreckers is the Shipwreck Historium. Here you will meet Asa Tift, one of the richest wreckers ever, and some of his fellow wreckers. The real life Asa Tift was a shipbuilder from Tifton, Georgia. When he wasn't chasing wrecks, he was a house builder.

One of Asa Tift's legacies is Hemmingway's House. He built it in 1851. Hemmingway acquired it at a tax sale for $8,000 in 1931. Here he penned many of his most famous works. He had an office built over the garage so he could work in peace. Maybe he needed a break from all his cats. He had hundreds, most six-toed cats, and their descendents are living the good life still in the house museum, Papa may still be working in his office too because many people have seen him wave to them from the window when no one was in the place.

Another well-known wrecker was Captain Francis Watlington. He and his wife Emmeline lived in Key West's oldest surviving house. The house was built in 1829 and occupied by the Watlington from about 1834. It is carefully preserved as a house museum. The Watlington's had nine daughters. Two of them died at a very early age and it is rumored Emmeline is still here caring for her two daughters. Sometimes the girls can be seen or heard playing marbles upstairs. And Emmeline's rocker will creak back and forth.

Another famous old home that still harbors a resident from another era is still another wrecker's home. In the 1840's, Captain John Hurling Gieger built himself what was believed to be the finest house in Key West. He and his wife, Lucretia, had twelve children. In that era, it was a sad fact that few families ever saw all of their children live to adulthood. So, too, the Geiger's. One of the upstairs rooms is obviously a child's room yet it has such a somber feel to it. The docent will tell you it was once used as a quarantine room during a yellow fever epidemic. Part of the emanations comes from a strange painting of a little girl. In those days, pictures called oil-a-grams were commissioned after a child died to have a likeness to remember him or her as he or she was. The deceased child would be propped up and painted. The artist always had a challenge to paint the eyes to look lifelike. It is believed that the disturbing portrait was one such picture. The docent in the home told me it was hung in the children's room where you could only see it from the mirror because it seemed to cause such problems when hung anywhere else. Perhaps the poor child's spirit wants to be in her own room, not the hall.

Finding Florida's Phantoms

She is not alone in the house. Docents and others have seen a middle-aged woman dressed in blue in the house. She just vanishes in front of your eyes.

The home had a distinguished guest in 1832. The man who gave the house the name it is known by today, John James Audubon. Visitors have also seen the famous artist in the house as well. One man visiting in 1963 saw the artist dressed in 19th century finery and was able to observe him for minutes before he slowly dissolved.

Even the bricks in the courtyard were once used as grave markers. Is it any wonder this house has such a haunted feel?

Not everyone in Key West was wrecker in the mid 1800's. Francisco Marrero was a prominent cigar maker in 1889 when he built the elegant home that is now the Marrero Mansion Guest House. He had a reason for building such a magnificent structure. He hoped to lure his young sweetheart to Key West. Marrero's ploy worked even better than he dreamed. However, Francisco had a dark secret that he never told Enriquetta even after years of marriage and several children. It wasn't not until he suddenly died on a business trip to Cuba that she found out the shocking truth. He had a first wife in Cuba that he had never divorced. That gave this legal wife, Maria Garcia de Marrero, ownership not only of the house Enriquetta loved but also of all Francisco's assets. Enriquetta was thrown out into the street to survive as best she could. As she was being evicted, she stated, "As God is my witness, I will always remain here in spirit."

Remain she did to this day. Owners and guests in the bed and breakfast say her spirit still looks after the home she loves in life and lets her displeasure be known if anyone she feels is unsuitable enters the home. She dislikes anyone who is grumpy or has a disagreeable nature. One way she lets this be known is by the crystal chandelier in the entryway. If it begins to sway when a guest enters, the owners know that person will probably be checking out shortly. Several people in the guesthouse have even seen her.

Now the Red Rooster is a horse of a different color, or perhaps I should say a bird of a different feather. It was originally built by a man named Delgado. He also was in the cigar business. People believed that he and his wife was a happily married couple so when Mrs. Delgado told friends one October day that her husband had gone to Cuba on business, no one was too concerned. When he never returned, people believe he may have died there or perhaps abandoned his wife and did not want to be found. No one thought any more about it until Mrs. Delgado confessed on her deathbed to killing him and burying the body under the house somewhere. The body could never be found but passersby still refer to the cement block porch as the largest tombstone in town.

Over the years the home housed several generation of the Delgado family, then became a low rent apartment complex for military personal and for a time was called The Cinderella Motel. As the name hints, it was little more than a brothel.

Today, the house is The Red Rooster Inn. The present owner has named and decorated the rooms in honor of local drag queens. So don't be surprised to find yourself staying in a roomed called "Patty Cake" or "La La Bella."

Don't be surprised either to find a cigar smoking Cuban gentleman smoking a fragrant cigar and staring soulfully at you in your room. Perhaps he is trying to tell you where his body is buried.

Kathleen Walls

Key West has its own version of a haunted "skyscraper." The La Concha Hotel, at seven stories, is the tallest building on the island. That is part of the reason it has its own resident spook. A technician working on the elevator one day accidentally stepped into the shaft and plunged to his death. Guest will be tapped on the shoulder and turn to see who is there. No one is present, physically at least. This is also a good place to sit on the rooftop bar and enjoy a sunset if for some reason you don't want to see it from Mallory Square. Of course, Sunset at Mallory square must be seen at least once. It is the biggest free entertainment in town. You will find jugglers, psychics, masseurs, tightrope walking dogs and cats who leap through flaming hoops - and that's just the start of what you may see at the square at sunset.

Perhaps Key West's best known haunting involves Robert the Doll. Robert Eugene Otto, a painter who was born in the Artist House in 1900, got the doll as a child. Robert blamed it for everything bad that happened to him. It was given to him by a Bahamian servant girl, who along with her family, worked for the Otto's. It is believed that the little girl put a curse on the doll as some type of payback for something the boy had done to her. The first thing Robert did was give his name to the doll. From that day on, the doll was called "Robert" and the boy only answered to "Gene." Whenever anything bad happened, Gene blamed Robert. Gene left the house for a while but returned and brought his bride, Anne, there. Anne was a classical pianist while Gene was an artist. He used the attic as his studio and Robert kept him company there. He even built furniture for the doll in the attic. People who visited found the grown man's preoccupation with the doll strange. The found the doll even stranger. People swore it moved around the attic by itself and peered out windows when Gene wasn't there.

The doll, dressed in a white sailor suit, remained in the attic for years after Otto died in 1974. Anne left the house then, leaving Robert behind in his attic room. The house was leased with the stipulation that Robert be undisturbed in his room.

After Anne's death, the house became The Artist's House Bed And Breakfast. Robert was moved to East Martello Museum. It has been confirmed by visitors and custodians alike that Robert has been known to move around his glass case. He apparently does not like to be photographed and has drained batteries, disabled cameras and ruined film to avoid having his picture taken.

Through the years, Key West has been a magnet to draw visitors from the cold north. Both the wealthy and the poor, the unknown and the famous have come to this island kissed by sun and sea. One of the best-known visitors was President Harry Truman. His Key West home is known as The Little White House. It was built in 1890 as the first officer's quarters on the naval station. Originally a wooden duplex, it was converted into a single-family dwelling in the beginning of the 20th century. Truman came here first in 1946 and returned ten additional times to his "Winter White House." The home is still furnished much like it was in the late 1940's. Other presidents, Dwight Eisenhower, John Kennedy and Jimmy Carter have also visited it.

But there is another presence there. An evil entity. Its presence has caused several employees to quit their jobs rather than be confronted by "it" another day.

Finding Florida's Phantoms

Of course, you come to expect ghosts in cemeteries. Key West won't disappoint you there. There are too many to count. Some of the saddest ones are of the children. They died in a deliberately set fire when the pastor of a church located just across the alley caught his wife cheating with the church's deacon. He set fire to the church during a Sunday school class. People claim to hear the children laughing and playing near the stature of the angel. They will become upset if you smoke in the cemetery.

Another spirit is considered very angry. He causes the trees nearby to blow around frantically when there is no wind. He is believed to be one of the people who drove out the pirates from Key West.

As you have already heard, all of Key West's dead are not in the cemetery. A victim of one of the strangest cases of all times may or may not be buried in the cemetery. The story of Elena Hoyos and the deranged count makes Ed and his Coral Castle seem like an Ozzie and Harriet relationship by comparison.

Elena Milagro Hoyos Mesa was the beautiful young daughter of a Cuban family who had fallen on hard times. Count Carl Tanzler von Cosel was a self-styled nobleman and medical practitioner. He went to Key West around 1930 and worked as an x-ray technician in the Marine Hospital. It was there that he met Elena. She was dying of tuberculosis. Although Carl had a wife and children on the mainland, he wanted to marry Elena. Since she was a staunch Catholic and was already married to a man who had deserted her when her illness became apparent, she refused.

Nonetheless, when she died in 1931, Carl offered to provide a handsome mausoleum for his beloved. He had it equipped with a phone so he could "talk" to her. About eighteen months after she died, he could stand it no longer. He went to the grave at night and dug up her decomposing corpse. He brought her body back to a small house he had on Flagler Ave.

There, using a combination of medical procedures, embalming techniques, wax and plaster of Paris, he "reconstructed" Elena. He dressed her in a wedding dress and considered her his bride. In 1940, he was discovered in bed with the body. He was considered sane and tried but never imprisoned.

The body of Elena was once again laid out at the funeral parlor. Thousands came to gawk. The distraught family hired three men to cut her body in three parts and bury them secretly so no one could ever desecrate her again. To this day, no one knows where she rests. In 1946, he wrote his memoirs and died in 1952 at age 75. In his memoirs, Cosel admitted that he often kissed Elena's body. However, in 1972, a doctor who had examined the corpse after it was retrieved revealed that the count had also had sexual relations with the corpse.

And that just scratches the surface of all the weird things in Key West. Many other places have rumors of hauntings. Ocean Key Resort, Cypress Inn and Eaton Lodge are some but the list is endless. Remember part of what makes Key West such a fascinating place to visit is the character of the city but even more so, it is the characters in the city.

Kathleen Walls

Contacts:

Sloppy Joe's 201 Duval St, Key West, Fl 33040
sloppyjoes.com/sloppys.htm
Captain Tony's
Address: 428 Greene Street
Phone: (305) 294-1838

BO's Fish Wagon
Corner of Caroline & William
05-294-9272
www.clydeskeywest.com/a%20save%20a/bos_fish_wagon.htm

Schooner Wharf Bar and Grill
202 William Street - Key West, Florida 33040
 305-292-9520
www.schoonerwharf.com/

Jimmy Buffett's Margaritaville, 424A Fleming St, Key West, FL 33040
Office: 305.296.9089 Fax: 305.296.1084
Toll Free order number 1.800.COCOTEL (262.6835)
http://margaritaville.com/

Marrero Mansion Guest House
410 Fleming Street ~ Key West, Florida 33040
(800) 459-6212 ~ (305) 294-6977 ~ Fax (305) 292-9030
info@marreros.com
www.marreros.com/

Red Rooster Inn
709 Truman Avenue, Key West, FL 33040
(305) 296-6558 (800) 845-0825
Fax: (305) 296-4822
info@redroosterinn.com
http://chelseahousekw.com/rooster/news.htm
The East Martello Museum and Gallery
3501 S. Roosevelt Blvd.
Key West,

305-296-3913

http://www.kwahs.com/

Little White House Museum - 111 Front Street, Key West (Truman Annex)
305- 294-9911. www.TrumanLittleWhiteHouse.com

The Artist's House
Eaton St.
(3050 296-3977

You are apt to find just about anything in Key West
Photo by Martin Walls

Top: The living room of the Audubon House
Bottom: Hard Rock Cafe, once Robert Curry's home
Photos by Martin Walls

Finding Florida's Phantoms

Credits:

Daytona Beach Ghost Tales That Never Die, Compiled and edited by Cheryl Atwell
Haunt Hunter's Guide to Florida, Joyce Elson Moore Pineapple Press
Haunting Sunshine, Jack Powell Pineapple Press.
Oldest Ghosts, Karen Harvey Pineapple Press
Ghosts of St. Augustine, Dave Lapham Pineapple Press
The Longstreet Highroad Guide to the Florida Keys & Everglades, Rick Farren
Ghosts of Key West, Davis L. Sloan Phantom Press
Ghosts Legends and Folklore of Old Pensacola, Sandra Johnson & Leora Sutton
Coast to Coast Ghosts: True Stories of Hauntings Across America, Leslie Rule
History of Jacksonville, Florida, and Vicinity, Thomas Frederick Davis
Greg Parker, Interview on Ashley's of Rockledge
Cheryl Atwell, Halifax Museum Director Interview
Joan Meyers, Personal Assistant Halifax Museum Interview
John Stenko, Artistic and Technical Director Daytona Playhouse, Interview
Bonnie Moreland, Interview on Seven Sisters Inn
Katie Mulhearn, Ocala Marion County Chamber of Commerce
Amanda S. Marcum, Carrabelle FL Unpublished document on Carrabelle
Welheim Bogan, Chef/Owner of Dock on the Bay Interview
Laura Justice, Interview on Doc. Sloan's house/CVS
Dr. S. Joseph Nassif, Director of Fine and Performing Arts at Rollins College. For interview on Annie Russell
Robert Zeman, Dunedin, FL Interview
Chelsea Mihall & Henry de la Vega of www.geocities.com/chelbell0485/WeirdAndFreakyTarpon/ Interview on Tarpon Springs
Bill Boyd, Interview about Harry's St Augustine
David Angier, The News Herald articles
Marlene Womack, The News Herald articles
Pricilla Goudreau, The Business Journal of Jacksonville
Timothy Allen Gilmore, The Business Journal of Jacksonville
Kristina Koehler, Jacksonville Times Union Online Shoreline
Bev Lonergan, Interview on St. Francis Inn
Kerry Sulivan, Interview on Scarlett's and O.C. White's
Shannon O'Toole, (The Ghost Hostess) The Original St Augustine Ghost Tours
Bill Harris, Interview on Hunter Arms
Margie Payne, Interview on Hunter Arms
Vickie Mullin, Interview on Hunter Arms
Jonathan Hay of Audio Stepchild for Interview on Studio 420 in Tarpon Springs
Clay Terrell. Interview on Peace and Plenty Inn
Connie Goodwin-Schwartz, Interview on Penny Farthing Inn
Kelly Ernest, Interview on Tampa
Tina Guillotte, Interview on St. Augustine Lighthouse

Pam Troll, Interview on St. Augustine Lighthouse
James Graves, Interview on Pensacola
Dwight Wilson, Jacksonville Beaches Areas Historical Museum Interview
Tara Schroeder, Interview on Tampa Theater
Shamus Hannigan, Interview on Ybor City
Ellen and Arthur Sturges, Interview on Chef Arthur's
Keven McGinn, Interview on Merl Kelce Library
Karen Mueller-Bryson Interview on Tampa
Helen Tasin, Interview on Ybor City
Emily Crumb, Interview on Flatauer House
David Butler, Interview on Flatauer House
Susan Owen, Interview on Don Cesar
Kathleen Gaye, Interview on Safty Harbor Spa
Florida Finacial News and Daily Record
Ocala Star Banner and Starbanner.com
www.crazedfanboy.com/ La Floridiana by William Moriaty Nolan
www.hollowhill.com,
www.orlandodiscovered.com,
www.cassadaga.org.
www.subversiveelement.com/Flight401EasternAirLines.html
www.geocities.com/donuts13/main_9.htm
www.ghosttracker.com
www.shadowland.com

www.ingramcontent.com/pod-product-compliance
Lightning Source LLC
Chambersburg PA
CBHW032046150426
43194CB00006B/441